FOREVER YOUNG

The Complete Anti-aging Programme

DR. SILKE HELLER   WERNER WALDMANN

FOREVER YOUNG
THE COMPLETE ANTI-AGING PROGRAMME

DUMONT monte

Conception and realisation: MediText, Stuttgart
Text: Dr. Silke Heller, Werner Waldmann
Translation: Debora Rebsch
Copy editing: Andrew Leslie
Layout: Karolina Stuhec Meglic
Photographs: Adobe Image Library (42); CMA (1); Corbis Images (2); Digital Stock (10); Digital Vision (14); Goodshoot (3); Image 100 (6); Image Source (1); John Foxx (2); Kaldewei (1); MEV (2); Photo Alto (20); Photo Disc (44); Stockbyte (2); Werner Waldmann (76)
Data management: DDS Lenhard, Stuttgart

Printing: Appl, Wemding (Germany)

© 2001 DuMont Buchverlag, Köln
(Dumont monte, UK, London)

The advice given in this book has been subjected to careful consideration and examination by the author, the editors and the publishers; nevertheless, no guarantee can be given. No liability can be assumed by the author, the editors, the publishers or their agents for personal injury, material damage or financial loss.

ISBN 3-7701-7028-8
Printed in Germany

The Dream of Eternal Youth

Ever since the dawning of humankind, people have been plagued by one of the great problems of existence itself – transience. This has led to a longing for eternal youth and the desire to delay aging as long as is humanly possible.

For as long as we are young and beautiful and our body continues to support us throughout all the adventures of our lives, we do not waste any time thinking about growing old. Besides, we tend to cross the threshold between 'young' and 'old' without realising it. Because no one visibly ages from one day to the next, we get used to the creeping process of physical deterioration – until one day we look in the mirror and see some sign of growing old or some small physical shortcoming gradually begins to annoy us.

The Devil Gives us Eternal Youth

In literature the subject of eternal youth, which is often symbolised by making a pact with the devil, is a very old motif. But research is hard on the heels of the causes of aging and each day we read in the newspaper that it will not be long before we can put a stop to the process in which our cells gradually die off. This hope must be like honey in the mouths of the many people who have fallen victim to the mania of youth. However, what the consequences for society would actually be if every one of those dreams were to become reality is generally not taken into consideration. A race of immortals in which people only die through accidents or sickness – but no longer as a result of growing old.

When we examine the situation closely we realise that medicine has given us a life expectancy that would have been almost unthinkable in past centuries. Becoming old most certainly does not have to mean simply bidding farewell to active life once and for all. Fortunately, modern medicine is able to delay illness-related death and extend the lifespan of elderly people by many years. It is surely down to the doctors that people have the opportunity of becoming older than ever before. However, classical medicine is more a type of repair medicine. Many illnesses which in the past would certainly have led to the patient dying sooner or later can now be cured easily.

Today, young people frequently find it difficult to believe that our ancestors died from what these days are regarded as minor ailments such as appendicitis, tuberculosis or influenza. These days, even serious illnesses like cancer or AIDS can be kept reasonably well under control and the patients often live for many years after the initial treatment.

Many of our contemporaries live to a ripe old age in spite of the fact that they suffer from some little problem or other. These days, despite the capacities of modern medicine, becoming old often means suffering from some chronic illness, which does not exactly improve the quality of life. This is a result of our lifestyle: stress, bad nutrition, and a lack of movement.

Anti-aging Means Strengthening the Body's Self-healing Powers

Anti-aging has become a buzzword that can mean all sorts of things. The philosophy comes from the US and describes a way of life that attacks the natural deterioration that accompanies aging. This idea has nothing to do with simply stopping time in its tracks and remaining eternally young. The anti-aging movement is based on the idea of managing one's mental and physical life in such a way that the body is continuously supplied with balanced quantities of all the vital nutrients that it needs to handle potential illnesses or even nip them in the bud on its own. In the most favourable scenario, the right nutrition can even replace the doctor to a great extent.

Although in the western industrialised nations we are not lacking food, we do often suffer from a deficiency of important nutrients. Vitamins, minerals, micro-nutrients, hormones and active vegetable ingredients have to be fed to the body through judiciously selected foodstuffs or as supplements to our diet. And then there is water: it is hard to believe, but most of us do not drink enough fluids. This is a simple matter to remedy, as our bodies only require water.

Lack of movement is the end of all life. Our bodies therefore require regular physical and mental activity. The daily walk to the office and shopping in the supermarket are not enough – you have to systematically challenge and encourage your body with sport and exercise. The same applies to the brain: those of us endowed with a natural thirst for knowledge have a good chance of staying alert in old age. Again, this does not mean routine work in our day-to-day working lives. People who read a lot and engage in lively discussion are well on the way to remaining young. This also includes always looking to the future rather than living in the past; in other words, being able to accept new developments. Mental fitness also includes social contact. We continuously have to grapple with the problems of others, especially older people. There is a good reason why we say that those who involve themselves with young people stay young themselves. This also applies to the joys of sexuality.

This book will show you how to discover strengths that you never realised you had; it can offer help in examining and if necessary changing your eating habits and can show you when you should take food supplements such as vitamins, minerals and micronutrients. It can help you decide whether it would be sensible to undergo hormone therapy; it will show you how to get your body back in shape through gentle training and how to discover hidden strengths through healthy exercise. And, finally, it will help you discover new joy of life by revitalising your relationship will your partner and by persistently training your grey cells.

CONTENTS

EAT WELL TO STAY YOUNG LONGER

The human organism has a fundamental need to be supplied with a nutritious diet. This is the only way it can remain healthy and fit and can protect itself against disease. And your general sense of well-being can also profit from lovingly prepared, tasty meals.

Eating – a Pleasure for Body and Soul

Normally, we don't think twice about our daily diet and simply fill up with food as we would fill up our cars with petrol. To make eating a real pleasure for body and soul, you shouldn't view it merely as a necessary evil but rather as a chance to give your body and soul a daily treat. This can be achieved quite easily:

- Take enough time to eat and enjoy your food, and don't simply reduce eating to a secondary activity beside watching TV or reading.

- Treat yourself to a nicely set table (ideally for every meal!) and make each meal a little highlight of everyday life.

- Eat slowly and chew your food thoroughly.

- Make your diet as varied as possible.

- Try new recipes and ingredients more frequently; use different herbs and spices (instead of salt) to season your meal.

- Eat fresh fruit and vegetables every day.

- Use oil sparingly.

- Don't eat too much meat or fish.

- Consume milk and dairy products regularly.

- Make use of wholemeal products.

- Cook meals mildly to preserve as many nutrients as possible.

- Make sure you drink enough fluids – at least $1^1/_2$ litres (3 pints) per day.

It is important to maintain a balance between the energy your body takes in and that which it uses up. This is why less is often in fact more.

On average, people in our latitudes consume at least 50% more calories than they actually need. Obesity has become one of the most serious dietary problems of industrial countries, and it reduces life expectancy. If you are too generous in your consumption of calories, this will have negative effects on your metabolism, unnecessarily strain your joints and increase your susceptibility to widespread geriatric illnesses such as diabetes. But if you do not consume more calories than your body really needs, you will delay the aging process.

Even though we are blessed with a surplus of food, we are repeatedly faced with deficiency symptoms which can also cause illnesses. A balanced diet based on your individual needs is therefore an indispensable basis for delaying the aging process and staying healthy and fit longer.

Everything you eat should be fresh, healthy, balanced and rich in nutrients. If sufficient amounts of these are available, you can rely upon a phalanx of active substances to strengthen your body's immune system, protect it from illnesses and keep it fit in the battle against the aging process. If your diet lacks one or more nutrients for an extended period of time, you are withholding important substances from your body and it won't be able to function properly.

The Most Important Anti-aging Nutrients

A well-functioning immune system and an inherent defence mechanism against all kinds of diseases are, as it were, fundamental features of the human organism. An unbalanced diet can easily cause this intricate self-defence mechanism to go off the rails. The diet of most people in industrial countries could be summed up in the words 'too much, too sweet and too fatty'.

Our body can deal with such maltreatment for an amazingly long period of time. However, with increasing age it also loses part of its ability to extract and absorb the nutrients necessary for its health from our diet. Less gastric acid is produced and gradually fewer nutrients such as folic acid or calcium are absorbed into the organism through our intestines. If you reduce your intake of dairy products with progressing age (perhaps because of intolerance of dairy products – a widespread ailment), your calcium intake is dramatically reduced. Now, at the latest, is the time to change to a healthy and balanced diet to ensure that your body can fight 'enemies' from within and without.

The examples given above aren't intended to intimidate you, but rather to demonstrate that your diet becomes more and more important with increasing age, and that it should guarantee the (urgently) necessary supply of nutrients and micro-nutrients.

A further example: so-called free radicals, which are aggressive waste products of oxygen metabolism, harm your body cells and expedite the aging process. A free radical is a molecule that is missing an electron. Being incomplete in this respect, it tries to restore itself by 'stealing' an electron from another, intact molecule. Its preferred prey are our body cells, which suffer lasting damage and as a result age prematurely.

Our body has a specific defence mechanism to ward off these substances, but the older we get, the more free radicals move through our body. The more you supply your body with 'radical hunters' (e.g. the antioxidant vitamins C and E, beta-carotene, folic acid, zinc and selenium), the greater is your chance of slowing down the aging process. This means that you're not helplessly exposed to these processes, but can actively contribute to your health.

The table opposite shows some of the most important anti-aging nutrients and their recommended daily allowances (RDA).

What do the various nutrients do for our body? Individually, they each bring about a variety of benefits which can complement each other and even increase the overall effect when combined carefully. The more balanced and complete the supply of nutrients is to your body, the more effectively you can prevent the aging process. In the following paragraphs, you can find some more details about the principal nutrients of the anti-aging diet.

VITAMIN C or ascorbic acid not only protects the body cells against attacks from free radicals, but a regular supply also reduces the risk of cardiovascular diseases by reducing the amount of harmful LDL-cholesterol (low-density lipoproteins) and increasing the amount of 'good' HDL-cholesterol (high-density lipoproteins) in our blood. Vitamin C slows down the calcification of the blood vessels, strengthens the cell membranes and can lower

Recommended Daily Allowances at a Glance

Nutrient	RDA		Comments
	For women	For men	
Beta-carotene	30 mg	40 mg	More intensive when taken with a little oil
Vitamin C	300 mg	400 mg	Vitamin C should be taken throughout the day. Smokers have a much higher demand.
Folic acid	0.4 mg	0.4 mg	Women taking the pill: 0.5 mg
Vitamin B_{12}	1 μg	1 μg	
Vitamin B_6 [1]	30–50 mg	30–50 mg	
Co-enzyme Q 10 [2]	30 mg	30 mg	With cardiovascular diseases: 50–70 mg
Vitamin E	100–150 mg	100–150 mg	
Glutathione	50–500 mg	50–500 mg	
Calcium	1.2 mg	1.2 mg	
Magnesium	400 mg	400 mg	When under a lot of stress or unusual physical strain: up to 700 mg
Selenium	150–300 μg	150–300 μg	A sufficient supply through your diet is basically impossible in our latitudes. A supplement is recommended.
Zinc	15–30 mg	15–30 mg	75 years and older: 50 mg

1) from age 40 onwards; 2) from age 50 onwards

blood pressure. It is also a valuable support for the immune system, since it stimulates the production of white blood cells. Moreover, because vitamin C can bind carcinogenic substances such as nitrosamine, it protects against cancer. A sufficient supply of Vitamin C can also prevent cataract and other eye complaints and is also good for the skin, connective tissue and gums.

Smokers especially have an immense need for Vitamin C, since it is destroyed by smoking. Vitamin C cannot be stored in the body; it should therefore be taken in small, regular doses spread throughout the day. This is effected by depot tablets, for example, which gradually release the vitamin into the organism over a period of several hours. Good sources of Vitamin C are citrus fruits, berries (especially strawberries and blackcur-

Vitamin E is an indispensable multi-talent when it comes to preventing or delaying age-related complaints.

rants), rose hip, buckthorn, peppers, asparagus, spinach, tomatoes, parsley and all types of cabbage.

Vitamin E or tocopherol is not only an efficient hunter of radicals. A sufficient supply of this vitamin reduces the risk of cardiovascular disease, especially arteriosclerosis, and helps prevent thrombosis. It is also supposed to be a barrier against some forms of cancer. It improves the efficiency of our brain, promotes blood production, stimulates our immune system and strengthens the connective tissues. Vitamin E also reduces the risk of cataract and is a useful weapon against rheumatism.

This versatile vitamin can be found in linseed, vegetable and fish oils, nuts, pine and sunflower seeds, eggs, seafood, leafy vegetables, avocados, broccoli and soy products.

Vitamin B$_6$ or pyridoxine plays an important role in the metabolic processes of the brain. Vitamin B$_6$ not only delays the decline of our memory but can even improve it and the overall efficiency of our brain. Furthermore, it increases the concentration of white blood cells, thereby strengthening our body's defences. Our daily requirement of Vitamin B$_6$ increases by about 20% as from the age of 40, after which our body can no longer absorb it from our food as efficiently. The principal sources of Vitamin B$_6$ are rice, pulse, potatoes, soybeans, nuts, wheat germ and wheat germ oil, all types of cabbage, fish and seafood, poultry products, peppers, bananas and avocados.

Our brain and nerve cells cannot function properly without a sufficient supply of **Vitamin B$_{12}$** or cyanocobalamin. A declining supply of this vitamin due the body's decreasing ability to absorb it (primarily after the age of 60) leads to a noticeable deterioration of mental capacities; a Vitamin B$_{12}$

deficiency can also cause psychological problems. Vitamin B_{12} plays an important role in blood production.

A large amount of Vitamin B_{12} is contained in animal products such as milk and dairy products, poultry, beef and veal, liver, fat fish (e.g. eel, salmon and tuna) as well as in beer, mushrooms and algae.

BETA-CAROTENE or pro-vitamin A is not only responsible for the appetising colour of carrots and tomatoes, but is an effective antioxidant that protects our cells from the attacks of the free radicals. A high level of beta-carotene is necessary to prevent physical and mental deterioration. A regular supply reduces the risk of cardiovascular diseases and cancer as well as preventing cataract. It also activates the immune system by boosting the efficiency and increasing the number of so-called killer cells, T-cells and lymphocytes which are needed for the body's inherent defence system. The principal sources of beta-carotene are all red and yellow fruits and vegetables, for example apricots, berries, carrots, tomatoes, peppers and chillies, as well as all types of cabbage (especially broccoli) and leafy vegetables, such as spinach or lamb's lettuce.

CALCIUM is the most important substance for our teeth and bones. With progressing age, the proportion of calcium in our bones is reduced; they become more frail and break more easily. This is why you should already consume a lot of calcium at a younger age. You'll eventually benefit from the depots you build up in your youth (the time of bone growth). Above and beyond this, calcium plays an important role in regulating your blood pressure, transmitting nervous impulses and providing stable cell membranes. A sufficient supply of calcium not only reduces the risk of osteoporosis but also protects you from cardiovascular diseases by reducing the percentage of unhealthy LDL-cholesterol in your blood. Important

In combination, beta-carotene, vitamin C and vitamin E are even more effective in protecting your cells against free radicals: as long as enough vitamin C is present, vitamin E has a stronger effect and beta-carotene is provided with some extra energy. This powerful trio can be found in broccoli, spinach and tomatoes.

sources of calcium are milk and dairy products (e.g. hard cheeses), but also wholemeal bread, nuts and almonds, all types of cabbages, green leafy vegetables, leeks, water cress, oranges and bananas, salmon, sardines and yeast.

MAGNESIUM is also an important nutrient that supports our body in quite a number of vital processes. It is imperative for the function of muscles (and therefore your heart), helps to build up natural body-inherent proteins and keeps your nerves in top shape. A good supply of magnesium can significantly reduce the risk of cardiovascular diseases, because it increases the amount of 'good' HDL-cholesterol in the blood and helps prevent platelets from clotting. It can also alleviate high blood pressure. Last but not least, magnesium is considered as a veritable 'anti-stress mineral' that has positive effects especially when you are under a lot of physical and mental strain. It can also be very helpful with nervousness, sleeping disorders and depression. Magnesium can be found in wholemeal products, pulses, green lettuces, milk and dairy products, bananas, dates, figs, nuts and almonds, sunflower seeds and pumpkin seeds, raisins, dried apricots, soy products, spinach, as well as in wheat germ, wheat bran and wheat germ oil.

Especially when you are under a lot of physical or mental strain, the 'anti-stress mineral' magnesium is a real relief.

FOLIC ACID, a vitamin of the B-group, protects against cardiovascular diseases by lowering the level of the protein homocystine in the blood. In highly concentrated form, this protein harms the blood vessels. A regular supply of folic acid reduces the risk of cancer and can afford protection against memory loss, lack of concentration, depression and dementia. A folic acid deficiency is often found in industrial countries – especially in pregnant women, women who have been on the pill for a long period of time, and elderly people. Folic acid is contained in green leafy vegetables such as spinach, lettuce and broccoli, but also in herbs such as parsley and water cress, in citrus fruits, artichokes, beetroot, tomatoes, cabbage, pulses, milk, liver and wholemeal products.

The CO-ENZYME Q10 not only protects the body against free radicals, but also has a key function in the respiratory process and plays a significant role in the production of adenosine triphosphate, which our body needs to produce energy. In addition, the co-enzyme Q10 is supposed to prevent the formation and growth of cancer cells. It strengthens the heart and other muscles and helps lower blood pressure. The increased heart rate has beneficial effects on the whole body. The human body is capable of producing the co-enzyme Q10 itself, as long as sufficient amounts of vit-

With advancing age, our body loses its ability to produce the important co-enzyme Q10. From the age of 50 onwards, you should start taking appropriate supplements.

amins B_{12} and B_6 as well as folic acid are available. Yet it loses this ability with increasing age, so that you should take a Q10 supplement from the age of 50 onwards. Co-enzyme Q10 can be found in fat fish, beef, eggs, peanuts, heart, liver and kidneys, wheat-germ oil and soy oil.

GLUTATHIONE, an amino acid compound, is an important part of the enzyme gluthathione-peroxidate, which can effectively protect you against free radicals: it can prevent their formation and disable existing ones, thereby preventing your cells from irreparable damage. It can also strengthen your body's defences and protects you against cardiovascular diseases, cancer and cataract. The human body can produce glutathione itself; a sufficient supply of Vitamin C and selenium will support and stimulate the production. A lack of glutathione can significantly speed up the aging process. To avoid this, you should regularly add carrots, asparagus, broccoli, cauliflower, Brussels sprouts, tomatoes, avocados and water melons to your diet.

ZINC stimulates the defences of your body's immune system. A zinc deficiency not only weakens your defences, but can cause premature aging of the body cells. A sufficient supply of zinc helps reduce the risk of cancer because it supports other nutrients in their battle against free radicals. To ensure a sufficient intake of zinc, your diet should frequently contain artichokes, wholemeal products, yoghurt, milk, eggs, poultry, nuts, wheat germ, fish, seafood, broccoli, sunflower seeds and pumpkin seeds.

An adequate supply of selenium can reduce the risk of cancer by as much as 50%.

The trace element SELENIUM has manifold ways of helping the body protect itself against premature aging. To put it simply, selenium prevents fats from going rancid in the cells and keeps these younger for a longer time. It disarms dangerous free radicals, strengthens the immune system and increases the body's resistance to illness. In addition, selenium can neutralise heavy metals such as mercury that accumulate in our organism. In doing so, it protects you against slow poisoning and the increased risk of cancer and arteriosclerosis. And what is more, selenium hinders the development of cancer cells.

A sufficient supply of selenium to the body can reduce the risk of acquiring cancer by as much as 50%. It cannot cure already existing cancer but can improve tolerance of the powerful medication used for its treatment. Whereas a young body can absorb selenium easily from food, this becomes increasingly difficult with advancing age. In addition, the plants in our latitudes have a fairly low level of natural selenium. According to estimates, most Europeans take in only about half of their required dose through their diet. This is why we recommend that you stock up your daily selenium supply with supplements. The most important natural sources of selenium are eggs, meat, lake fish and seafood, pulses, natural rice, sunflower seeds and oil, Brazil nuts, garlic and wholemeal products.

OMEGA-3 FATTY ACIDS are present in sufficient quantities in fish oils and garlic. When supplied regularly, they reduce the risk of cardiovascular diseases. They dilute the blood, help blood clots dissolve and reduce your blood pressure. They also keep the blood vessels lithe, increase the level of 'good' HDL-cholesterol and are supposed to reduce the incidence of metastasis production in cancer patients.

INVALUABLE REINFORCEMENTS FOR YOUR HEALTH

Besides these 'anti-aging specialists' there are a number of further nutrients that contribute towards keeping your body healthy. In the following paragraphs, you can read in what way these 'reinforcements' are useful, what they can do and in which foods they are to be found.

VITAMIN A, the 'eye' vitamin, strengthens your eyesight and keeps the skin and tissue healthy. It also helps in the battle against free radicals. Vitamin A is found in milk and dairy products, all yellow and orange fruits, green vegetables, liver and fish oils.

VITAMIN B$_1$ or thiamine keeps the sinews and muscles fit, stimulates the metabolism and strengthens your memory. It is to be found primarily in fish, beef and pork, soy products, natural rice, lentils, peas and wholemeal products. The tannin found in tea and coffee destroys Vitamin B$_1$. Even a slight deficiency can cause tiredness, headaches, lack of concentration, weight loss, depression and sleeping disorders.

We need **VITAMIN B$_2$** or riboflavin for more than just growing. It also plays a part in deriving energy from foods, gets the metabolism going and keeps your skin, tissue and mucous membranes healthy. It also contributes to the creation of blood cells. Vitamin B$_2$ can, for example, be found in dairy products, green leafy vegetables and meat. It is especially effective in combination with the vitamins B$_3$ and B$_6$.

A **Vitamin B₃** or niacin deficiency can lead to depression. Your body needs this vitamin to gain energy in the cells and to break down toxic substances, but also to process carbohydrates, fats and proteins and to build up cholesterol. It also supports the oxygen intake of the red blood cells. Our body can produce niacin itself from the protein tryptophan, which is why deficiencies are quite rare. Good sources of vitamin B₃ are meat, fish and seafood, poultry, nuts, grains and potatoes.

Vitamin B₅ or pantothenic acid is important for the metabolism of carbohydrates, fatty acids and amino acids as well as for the production of certain hormones and tissue. It is said to alleviate rheumatic complaint. You can find it in meat, eggs, soy and wholemeal products, nuts, beans and peas.

Vitamin D keeps your muscles and sinews fit and your bones resilient. It is contained for example in fat fish, milk and egg yolk. Our body can produce it itself when it is exposed to sunlight.

Our body needs **Vitamin H** for energy turnover and purification. Good sources are liver, eggs, beans, nuts, mushrooms, bananas and peas.

Vitamin K is indispensable for blood coagulation and healing processes. Apart from this, it keeps our bones and tissue healthy. It can be found e.g. in dark leafy vegetables, wholemeal products, dairy products and meat.

Copper is absolutely necessary for the health of our blood and bones. Your diet should therefore regularly include fish and seafood, liver, peas and nuts.

Our thyroid needs sufficient **iodine** to function properly, so you should use iodised salt and eat fish and seafood regularly.

An **iron** deficiency leaves you feeling exhausted and tired, and your fingernails will split. Your body primarily needs iron for blood production, since it is an important building block for the protein haemoglobin, which transports oxygen from the lungs to the cells. Your immune system also relies on a sufficient supply of iron. Green leafy vegetables, beef, poultry, nuts and beans are good sources of iron, as is red grape juice.

Potassium is significantly involved in the smooth functioning of the body's fluid balance and supports the functions of nerves and muscles. It reduces

Tea and coffee contain tannin, a substance that hinders the absorption of iron from food. That's why you should go without drinking tea or coffee for a few hours before and after eating foods containing iron.

water retention and alleviates high blood pressure. It also contributes to the production of body-inherent proteins and is capable of activating various enzymes. People who regularly drink large amounts of alcohol and those who eat very little fruit and vegetables tend to have a potassium deficiency; this can also be brought on by a diet which is very rich in salt. Possible negative effects are muscle weakness and constipation. Potassium is supplied by asparagus, bananas, apples, oranges, plums, beans, potatoes, wholemeal products, meat and fish, but also by the 'Indian potato' topinambour.

The 'Indian potato' topinambour has a special ingredient: inulin. This highly effective roughage lowers cholesterol levels, stimulates digestion and improves the natural balance of the intestines.

TASTY AND HEALTHY: WHAT SHOULDN'T BE MISSING FROM YOUR MENU

It is not necessary to design a complex diet in order to take in as many of these nutrients as possible. On the contrary, it is best if you combine a fairly wide variety of foods in your diet and eat a little of everything regularly.

Nature has a variety of foods in store for us that can contribute to our well-being in special ways. These foods, which can easily be incorporated into everyday cooking, will enrich your diet not only with regard to health but also in terms of taste. You should try to include one or more of the following foods in every meal.

**Why don't you try a tasty banana shake: Just put a banana, $^1/_4$ litre milk, some low-fat yoghurt and some cinnamon and honey through your food processor.
It's quick and tasty!**

Berries, cherries and grapes are rich in potassium, which is good for your blood pressure, and pectins, which help lower your cholesterol level. Strawberries, raspberries, cranberries and blueberries are veritable vitamin C wonders. These tasty miniature fruits not only taste delicious but are also highly efficient in the battle against radicals.

Let's stay in the fruit department: you should also frequently help yourself to citrus fruits such as oranges, lemons, mandarins, nectarines and grapefruit. Apart from a high level of vitamin C, potassium

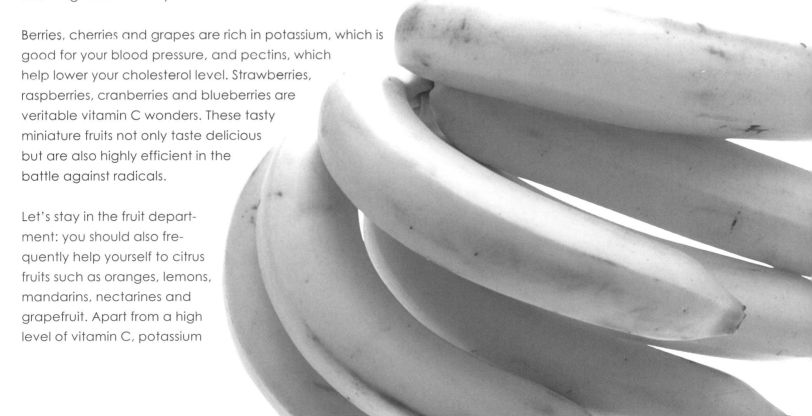

and pectin, these fruits have a variety of nutrients which can help your body fight the free radicals and the related premature aging.

Bananas are the ideal snack – naturally wrapped suitably for transport, they keep a large number of nutrients in store under their peel: sufficient vitamin B_3, B_6 and C and a lot of potassium, which lowers the blood pressure and is an important nutrient for elderly people.

Cabbage was long considered a poor man's food, but those times have long passed. In a lot of tasty variants, cabbage dishes regulate your digestion naturally. Rich in dietary fibres, this vegetable helps prevent cancer of the intestine. The various types of cabbage also supply your body

Many of the tomato's nutrients, among them lycopin, are heat-resistant. This means that tomato soup, ketchup, pureed tomatoes and tomato sauce are good sources of nutrients.

with calcium, potassium and many valuable antioxidants that keep your cells young and fit longer. Broccoli, for example, is a real multi-talent: apart from a lot of vitamin K it contains all important radical-killers in a highly effective combination. The pleasant side-effects are that your body cells are effectively protected and susceptibility to cardiovascular diseases and cancer is reduced. But cauliflower, Chinese cabbage and Brussels sprouts should also appear on your menu in regular intervals. In addition, green-leafed cabbages are good sources of iron which develop their full potential in combination with foods that are rich in vitamin C, such as peppers.

Does your mouth start to water at the sight of ripe bright red tomatoes? Go ahead – help yourself! The colorant lycopin which gives them their appetising bright colour is invaluable for your cells: it protects them against free radicals far more effectively than the related beta-carotene. This makes it a useful ally in the battle against cancer and cardiovascular diseases. Apart from lycopin, tomatoes contain large quantities of vitamin C, folic acid and beta-carotene.

Carrots are every bit as healthy as they look: the colorant beta-carotene which gives them their appetising colour also protects your cells against free radicals very effectively. It is assisted by vitamin C, of which carrots also contain a large amount. And that's not everything: the nutrients contained in carrots get your immune system going and lower the risk of cardiovascular problems. This is why carrots should frequently be on your menu – either raw to munch on between meals, as juice or as a vegetable side dish.

Green salads provide plenty of radical-killers and vitamins. In addition, green salad, especially lettuce, is supposed to lower the risk of cancer as well as stimulating the function of your liver and digestive system. Even though spinach has wrongly been claimed to be a good source of iron, this vegetable has a lot to offer – for instance a rich selection of nutrients that protect your body cells against the attacks of free radicals.

Peppers are another all-round talent; especially the red ones are full of vitamin C, E and beta-carotene. This trio gets rid of free radicals and thus effectively protects your cells against premature aging.

Artichokes are also a valuable weapon against old age. These edible thistle blossoms do not only contain an abundance of folic acid and zinc,

You should regularly eat green lettuce. It contains a lot of valuable nutrients – the outer dark leaves, by the way, contain more than the lighter-coloured inner ones.

which strengthen your immune system and keep your cells fit. They also support your digestion and stimulate your liver and gall bladder. In addition they can lower the level of harmful cholesterol in the blood and have a stabilising effect on your blood sugar level.

Avocados are a very good source of glutathione and vitamin E and are therefore an indispensable ally in the battle against free radicals. Further bonuses are their high level of unsaturated fatty acids and their positive effect on cholesterol levels. Avocados should be a regular part of your diet, either in salads or as spicy guacamole.

Soybeans are also powerful allies in the battle against premature aging. As well as containing a wealth of antioxidants, they are also rich in the substance genistin, which has a function similar to that of the body's hormone oestrogen. Not only does genistin relieve menopausal complaints; it is also suspected of lowering the risk of breast cancer and preventing blood clots.

A lot of the nutrients contained in garlic are not heat-resistant. Garlic should therefore be added towards the end of cooking, or used raw in salads and sauces. If you remove the green shoots, you can even keep the pungent smell to a minimum.

Of course, it is a myth that garlic protects you against vampires. On the other hand, it can protect you against real dangers, for example cardiovascular diseases and cell damage through free radicals. The pungent tubers contain a powerful mixture of nutrients which not only lower blood pressure, but also dissolve blood clots, prevent deposits from forming on blood vessel walls and keep the blood vessels flexible. In addition, garlic increases the level of good HDL-cholesterol in the blood, lowers that of the bad LDL-cholesterol and stimulates your immune system. Other onion-like plants – shallots, leeks, spring onions and chives – are good for the cardiovascular system. If you eat onions regularly, you will be more resilient against colds and respiratory complaints.

Chilli peppers are very powerful: capsicain, the substance that makes these peppers so hot, is a good weapon against carcinogenic substances. Capsicain also stimulates the production of endorphins in the body, which makes it an efficient stress-killer. This substance is also supposed to stimulate the circulation and reduce the risk of blood clots. Like many spicy foods, chilli stimulates your metabolism and its vitamin C content protects your cells from damage by free radicals.

Fat fish are excellent sources of omega-3 fatty acids.

Do you like fish? That's good! Fish should be served twice a week – ideally, those types of fish with a high fish oil content. By eating fish regularly you provide your body with highly potent omega-3 fatty acids, which lower

your blood pressure and cholesterol level and protect you against cardiovascular diseases. This is also true of seafood, which additionally provides your body with plenty of selenium and zinc – effective protection against premature cell aging.

Milk and dairy products can cover your body's requirements of valuable calcium and can simultaneously provide you with a lot of further nutrients. Yoghurt with live bacteria (especially those

Your cooking oil should be of a high quality, contain a lot of nutrients and be cold-pressed without chemical additives. When you buy olive oil, look for the expression 'olio extra vergine de oliva' or 'native olive oil extra'. Only high-quality oils are permitted to bear this label.

producing D-lactic acids) stimulates your digestion, helps keep the natural balance in the intestines and gets your immune system going.

If you like olive oil (and can tolerate it!), you should only use high-quality products. Olive oil contains a lot of polyunsaturated fatty acids and many antioxidants, which protect your body cells against free radicals and reduce the risk of cardiovascular diseases and cancer. Wheat germ oil is a good alternative to olive oil. It is especially rich in vitamin E, folic acid and unsaturated fatty acids.

You can also find powerful ingredients for your personal anti-aging diet amongst herbs and spices. Asian food would be inconceivable without ginger. But did you know that this aromatic tuber contains anti-inflammatory substances?

Having to crack tough nuts is not only good for your brain. Of course, we are not talking about riddles here, but about a highly nutritious snack. Nuts contain a lot of vitamin E along with many omega-3 fatty acids and keep your cells young. Brazil nuts are full of selenium, and the invaluable element magnesium is primarily contained in almonds and cashews.

Many people regard shoots and sprouts as the epitome of a healthy diet. Especially in winter, they really are a useful dietary supplement, because vegetables lose a lot of vitamins through long transport and storage. If you find it too arduous to grow your own on the window sill, you can just as well resort to fresh cress. The various types of cress have the effects of natural antibiotics and can safeguard against infectious diseases.

Are you highly stressed? Then you should relax with a cup of green tea every now and then. Its high vitamin B_1 content reduces the detrimental effects of stress. Green tea is a rich source of vitamin C, aromatic oils, tannin and minerals. It is said to prevent cancer, heart complaints and tooth decay, reduce blood pressure, blood sugar and cholesterol levels, and stimulate both your immune system and metabolism. It also has a general stimulating effect and increases your ability to concentrate.

Alternative medicine has provided us with ginkgo extracts and ginseng preparations. In Asian countries, ginseng is regarded as a veritable fountain of youth and is regarded as an aphrodisiac. Ginseng roots contain substances that invigorate the whole body. In Chinese medicine, the ginkgo tree has always been considered as a versatile medicine. Extracts from its

Green tea is made from dried tea leaves that have not been fermented additionally (as they are for black tea). A lot of nutrients are thereby preserved. If pure green tea is too strong for you, you might want to try mixtures of tasty fruit and green tea.

dried leaves are used against mental deterioration because they stimulate the circulation of the blood. They are used to combat the effects of memory disorders, stroke, heart attacks and arteriosclerosis. Ginkgo nutrients help defend the body against free radicals and prevent blood clots. Ginkgo is also prescribed against dizziness, buzzing in the ears and even tinnitus. According to popular medicine, ginkgo biloba seeds have an aphrodisiac effect.

To Your Health!

Alcohol and a healthy diet – are they compatible? Yes, as long as your consumption of alcohol remains within sensible limits. Scientific research has exonerated alcohol of its health-damaging reputation.

Apart from the fact that a glass of alcohol has a relaxing and invigorating effect on a lot of people, red wine in particular is a definite bonus to your health. The magic word is resveritrol: this substance is especially abundant in red grapes and thus in red wine. It lowers the level of damaging LDL-cholesterol, increases that of beneficial HDL-cholesterol and reduces susceptibility to thrombosis. But it has a lot more to offer besides these positive effects on your blood vessels: it stimulates your immune system, neutralises free radicals, gets your metabolism going and supports a number of enzymes in their battle against cancer.

Red wine contains about ten times as much resveritrol as white wine, because the red grapes are fermented with their nutritious skins whereas white wine is only made from the grape juice.

However, you shouldn't be drinking more than half a pint of red wine per day. And if you don't like red wine or can't tolerate it – fresh red grapes also contain resveritrol.

How to Ensure that Important Nutrients aren't Lost: Suggestions for Shopping, Storage and Preparation

A healthy diet begins with the selection of foods and their preparation. If you want to eat in a healthy way, you should not only focus on a balanced menu. To benefit the most from all nutrients, the following aspects should be considered when buying, storing and preparing food.

Take a close look at the fruit and vegetables that you buy, so you can be sure of obtaining absolutely fresh food. Pale and wilted fruit or vegetables have often been stored too long and contain only a fraction of their original nutrients. Deep-frozen vegetables provide a good alternative. They are frozen as soon as they are reaped, to ensure that their nutritional value remains at a high level. Ideally, fruit and vegetables should be supplied by guaranteed organic farms. Fruit should not be waxed, and citrus fruits not sprayed. A lot of supermarkets nowadays include organically grown products in their range.

In a lot of organic shops, you can get a weekly 'vegetable subscription' – a bag with a varied selection of the season's fresh organic fruits and vegetables.

A special service is now offered by quite a number of greengrocers: the so-called 'vegetable subscriptions'. If desired, they will make up a bag of the season's freshest fruits and vegetables – mostly from your local region – every week. A lot of organic farms also offer this type of subscription service and sometimes even deliver free of charge. This is an excellent way of getting a varied selection of fresh organic products at a stable price. Among these you will also find long-forgotten vegetables that have only recently been rediscovered for your diets, for example arugula, white turnips or mangel-wurzel. You can grow fresh herbs on your window sill or balcony yourself: they are rich in vitamins and a tasty supplement to many dishes.

When buying meat products, you should prefer those originating from free-range farming. A lot of organic farms sell meat and also offer 10 or 20 kilogramme packages containing various kinds of meat. This you can freeze in smaller portions.

Natural or organically grown products should invariably be preferred to synthetic ones, which are likely to have gone through various processing stages. Chose natural, real honey and not artificial honey, and unsweetened fruit juice rather than processed fruit nectar. When buying oil, you should really insist on high-quality cold-pressed oils. Vinegar should have been fermented organically; and buy fresh full-fat milk rather than long-life or sterilised products. Mild yoghurt or organic yoghurt with primarily D-lactic acids, which is made with bacteria such as lactobacillus bifidus or lactobacillus acidophilus, is highly beneficial to the balance of your intestine.

In general, it can be said that the shorter the time between reaping and consuming foods, the higher the level of nutrients remains. Broccoli, for example, loses about 5% of its vitamin C content per day when stored at room temperature. Because exposure to sunlight speeds up the loss of some vitamins, it is best to store fruit and vegetables in a cool, dark place (for example in the vegetable compartment of your refrigerator) before eating them.

Unfortunately however, a certain amount of nutrient loss is unavoidable during the processing and preparation of foods. On the other hand, that of course doesn't mean that you should only eat raw foods. It is not difficult to preserve valuable nutrients when preparing meals while at the same time creating something very tasty and appealing. If you follow a few basic rules while cooking, you can keep the loss of vitamins and minerals to a bare minimum.

When preparing food, you should stick to a simple rule of thumb: cook as quickly and as gently as possible. You should therefore use chopped fruit and vegetables immediately and not cook them longer than necessary.

All ingredients should be as fresh as possible. A lot of vitamins react sensitively to light and oxygen, and others are water-soluble. That's why you should wash fruit and vegetables briefly but thoroughly with a lot of water before cutting it up. If you let them soak in water too long, important nutrients are washed out. Scrub lettuce and vegetables only briefly. If you have to peel vegetables, try to remove only the top layer as thinly as possible. Many nutrients are to be found directly under the skin and if you are too enthusiastic while peeling, a lot of nutrients will end up in the bin – unused. Buy a vegetable brush: potatoes and carrots can be eaten with their skins once they are thoroughly scrubbed.

You should chop up you ingredients only if you are ready to use them immediately. A food processor not only saves you a lot of effort; it also slices and grates fruit and vegetables quickly, without unnecessary exposure to oxygen.

Vegetables that require a longer cooking time are best cut into small pieces, and those that don't take so long into larger pieces.

Make sure you use high-quality pots and pans: the lid must close tightly so that not too much steam escapes when simmering. Pots with double bottoms can conduct heat efficiently and evenly. A wok is also very versatile: foods can be cooked very quickly, which again preserves nutrients. Last but not least, you can use a microwave oven to prepare a lot of nutritious dishes easily and quickly.

The faster and the more carefully foods are cooked, the more nutrients are preserved. Because a lot of vitamins are water-soluble or sensitive to heat, you shouldn't cook vegetables longer than really necessary. Boil the water first, then add the vegetables and cook them briefly. Use the cooking water as a basis for gravy or soups, because it often contains a lot of water-soluble food elements.

Even milder than cooking in water is steam cooking. When doing this, you should also use the remaining liquids. Fresh herbs and vegetables, which are added to the food after steaming (or are only cooked briefly), round off the taste and supply further essential substances. When making vegetable soups, you can compensate for the heat-related loss of nutrients: don't cook all the vegetables, but add some raw vegetables, finely chopped or grated.

A nutrition-friendly way of preparing foods rich in protein, such as fish, meat and fibrous vegetables, is to braise or roast them. First, the foods are fried from all sides, then water is added before stewing the food in an enclosed pot at about 100 °C (212 °F) in the simmering liquid and steam. A little water is then added occasionally. The remaining meat juices (made from the sediment left by the roast and the added water) are the ideal basis for a tasty and nutritious gravy that contains a lot of flavour and nutritious elements (e.g. water-soluble vitamins, minerals and proteins). You should always use the meat juices to minimise the loss of nutrients.

Oils should not be brought to the boil; this could release substances that are detrimental to your health. That's why you should definitely turn down the heat before the oil begins to steam.

How to Get Rid of Bad Eating Habits

Does this sound familiar to you? Even though you eat at regular intervals, you feel listless and exhausted, have sudden cravings for sweets or drag yourself from one cup of coffee to the next. The reasons are probably to be found in your diet and your eating habits.

Even though most people take in more calories than their body needs to make it through the day, many of these calories are 'empty' and do not supply the body with the required nutrients. The typical diet in the Western world is rich in fats, salt and refined sugar, and lacks fibre. We also don't eat enough fruit and vegetables – all too often, the price for this is obesity or cardiovascular problems.

Actually, it is not very difficult at all to adapt your diet to your body's requirements. The simple formula is to eat the right food at the right time. Is your diet composed of the foods your body really needs? Or are you burdening your body with useless, empty calories, and is it perhaps lacking vital nutrients? The following checklist will help you to fully understand your eating habits.

Does your diet still show weaknesses? Then you should try to get rid of them little by little: don't radically change your eating habits from one day to the next, but do so gradually.

You will then form new habits and won't have the feeling that you suddenly have to go without certain foods. You will also be able to learn and prac-

Food is cooked very gently in steam. Sieves are available in most household goods shops or department stores. Fill a pan with about 3–5 cm (1^1/$_4$–2 inches) of water, bring this to the boil, put in the sieve, add the vegetables and let them simmer in the closed pan.

Check out Your Eating Habits!

What are your eating habits?
Tick the statements that are true for you
and then add up the ticks.

I eat fruit and vegetables at least
five times a day. ◯

I drink less than four cups of tea
or coffee a day. ◯

I eat less than four eggs per week. ◯

I only drink alcohol occasionally, and when I do,
only one glass a day. ◯

I eat mostly wholemeal bread and pasta. ◯

I try to keep my diet low in fat and, for example,
prefer skimmed milk and low-fat dairy products. ◯

Fish or seafood are on my menu at least
once a week. ◯

I drink at least 1$^1/_2$ litres (3 pints) per day:
primarily water, unsweetened herbal and
fruit teas and diluted juices. ◯

I tend to eat fruit and vegetables raw,
steamed or simmered. ◯

I very rarely eat fast food or ready-to-eat meals. ◯

I don't take sugar in my tea or coffee
and drink two glasses of lemonade or cola
per day at the most. ◯

At least twice per day, I have foods
that are rich in fibre, e.g. muesli, wholemeal
bread, fruit and vegetables. ◯

I try to buy freshly reaped products and to
eat them as soon as possible. ◯

I only consume animal fats (as are found
for instance in milk, meat, butter or cheese)
twice a day. ◯

EVALUATION:

0–4 ticks:

You know already that there is quite a lot wrong with your diet: too much fat and sugar and not enough nutrients and fibres – factors which you will pay for with a higher risk of disease and faster aging. Look at all the statements you didn't tick and see if you couldn't at least try to apply some of them. Remember: you're doing yourself and your health a favour if you change to a healthier, more balanced diet.

5–9 ticks:

You're on the right track! You're aware of the importance of a healthy diet and have already applied some important principles. To do your health a favour, you should now try to increase your endeavours towards a healthy lifestyle. The statements you haven't ticked can give you some valuable tips regarding some weak points in your diet that you can gradually rectify. To evaluate yourself, you can repeat this test from time to time to see if you've made further improvements.

10–14 ticks:

Congratulations! You have a healthy and balanced diet and are already doing a lot for your health. If you didn't tick all the statements, which ones didn't you tick? Maybe you should go back and check whether it might be worthwhile to optimise your eating habits in these respects – your health will thank you for it.

tise your new eating habits over a period of time until they become second nature to you.

A drastic change of diet could affect your well-being. If you change to a very fibrous diet from one day to the next, your digestive system won't be able to adapt as quickly and will react with flatulence or cramps.

However, it is not only important what you eat, but also when, why and how. Little in-between snacks used to be frowned upon because they were thought to spoil our appetite for the main meals. Nutritional science has now shown that a bite or two between meals can be beneficial.

The body's principal energy source is glucose, which our body obtains by processing carbohydrates. A low level of glucose in the blood lowers the productivity of the brain. Sensible power-snacks keep the blood sugar level stable and provide a regular supply of energy to the body. Five small meals a day are more readily digestible than three large ones.

Glucose is very quickly absorbed by our body cells. On the other hand, it is not sensible to feed your body sugary food as quick energy-boosters whenever you get tired. The invigorating effect does not last very long, because you set off a vicious circle in your body by having a chocolate bar, an ice-cream or crisps: the sugar is converted to glucose and your blood sugar level rapidly rises. This leads to an increased release of insulin. The sugar is broken down very quickly, your blood sugar level sinks rapidly, and soon you will feel exhausted and tired again and will get another craving for food.

The same rules apply to sensible power snacks as to nutritious meals: they should consist of fruit, vegetables, wholemeal or dairy products and be rich in fibre. A banana or a slice of wholemeal bread won't give you as quick an energy boost as a chocolate bar, but they will provide your body with a steady flow of energy for a longer period of time. And if it does have to be chocolate – have a power snack beforehand, so that your body can make use of the released insulin.

Whenever possible, you should take the time to eat slowly and to enjoy your food. A meal you wolf down standing up or while you're watching television or leafing through your business paperwork might stop you from feeling hungry, but it's not good for you. A nicely set table and an appetising meal, on the other hand, can be a nice relaxing break from the day's hustle and bustle. And why not turn your meals into little rituals: play some background music, light a candle... simply relax! You should feel good while eating.

However, this doesn't mean that you should eat whenever you feel bad. Stress, worries and anger are not the best of guests to have along for dinner: they tend to make you oblivious to the real needs of your body. Of course, you can treat yourself occasionally with a chocolate bar or a piece of cake; but make sure that you are consciously treating yourself, and don't let these exceptions become the rule.

Foods that you eat with a positive attitude and appetite are better for your body than those you stuff yourself with out of frustration or boredom. Some kinds of 'hunger' can only be numbed by foods for a short time, but can't be satisfied. Sudden cravings should arouse your suspicion: try to find out if food really helps. If it doesn't, then do yourself a favour and fill the 'void' with the right substance. Maybe your body (or your soul) just needs some 'TLC', some exercise or is simply asking for a diversion from a tiring or boring task.

THE SENSE AND NONSENSE OF FAD DIETS

Hardly a day goes by without a new fad diet being promoted that promises miracles: hard-boiled eggs, pineapple, bananas, dry bread rolls – there are countless diets around. Some do in fact bring about a rapid weight loss, but this effect rarely lasts for a long time. They can actually put a strain on your body: such one-sided diets basically promote a variety of deficiency symptoms.

If you really want to lose weight, you will have to change your diet and ideally take up some kind of sport. If you are not prepared to do so, a healthy and long-lasting weight reduction will remain an illusion; after all, it is no secret that there is a close connection between eating, movement and weight.

Whatever you eat must be burnt up either through physical activity or heat production. If you use up more energy than you take in, you will lose weight. If your energy expenditure is lower than your intake, your body will store

Diuretics are absolutely unsuitable in supporting a diet. Losing water means losing weight, and the necessary reduction of fat is omitted. You should also stay away from pills that block your appetite. Many of these pills which allegedly help you lose weight quickly and easily are based on the idea of filling your stomach: the tablet absorbs liquid in your stomach and swells. Such methods do not help you reduce your weight permanently because they don't change the cause of your weight problem: your bad eating habits.

the excess energy as a fat deposit. Your body only uses up as much energy as it really needs to keep the metabolism and bodily functions going. This is called BMR (basal metabolic rate) and depends on your age, sex and level of physical activity.

You can't fool your body with crash diets: it will react to a sudden dramatic reduction of food intake by lowering the BMR – you body then starts running low and constantly signals its need for nutrition. You'll be hungry all the time and soon give up your diet out of sheer frustration. Lasting results can only be achieved by eating sensibly and increasing your level of physical activity.

Before you seriously attempt to lose weight, however, you should find out whether you do in fact weigh too much (see feature "Are you really too fat?" on pages 32/33). The model of feminine beauty, as presented in advertisements and the media, has basically nothing to do with the healthy reality. Of course, some of the slim, long-legged models may be nice to look at. But from a medical point of view, a lot of them have a serious underweight problem – and this can be just as dangerous and harmful to your health as weighing too much.

Losing Weight Starts in Your Head: Getting and Staying Slim

You really do weigh too much and would like to lose a bit of weight? Fine! But go about it slowly. It is not very sensible to be constantly thinking about losing weight or being overly ambitious. So avoid the bikini-figure-in-five-days diet and similarly radical sudden cures. Diets such as these only have the feared yo-yo effect.

If you want to lose weight in a sensible manner and make these effects last, you will really have to make fundamental changes to your diet. It is also much healthier for your body to lose weight gradually over a few months than to lose a lot very rapidly. If you stop providing your body with carbohydrates from one day to the next, that will upset the balance of electrolytes in your body or – if worst comes to worst – even lead to palpitations or a stroke. If your diet lacks protein, your body could compensate by breaking down its own proteins contained in the muscles and the heart to an increasing extent.

The change between radical weight loss during a diet and rapid weight gain afterwards is called the 'yo-yo effect'. Often, you weigh more after a diet than you did before. The yo-yo effect occurs frequently with repeated crash diets, and is very exhausting for the organism. Also, your body 'learns' that it isn't always provided with sufficient food and is then more reluctant to part with its fat reserves, which it prefers to retain in order to tide us over during hard times.

ARE YOU REALLY TOO FAT?

There are various methods of determining the ideal weight of an individual. The so-called 'standard weight according to Broca' is considered rather dated nowadays. However, this method is quite useful to give you a rough idea. You can determine your standard weight according to Broca by using the following formula:

Height (in cm) minus 100 = standard weight in kg

For example, if you are 168 cm (5' 6") tall, your standard weight – according to this, would be 68 kg (150 pounds). If you weigh more, you are probably slightly overweight. But this is no reason to get worried.

Nowadays, the so-called body mass index (BMI) is used to determine whether you are overweight or not. The BMI gives you information about the amount of fat present in the body. It is calculated as follows:

Weight (in kg) ÷ height (in m)^2

So if you are 168 cm (5' 6") tall and weigh 70 kg (154 pounds), your BMI would be
70 ÷ (1.68 x 1.68) = 24.8

So, what does this number mean? The World Health Organisation (WHO) has defined overweight and obesity as follows:

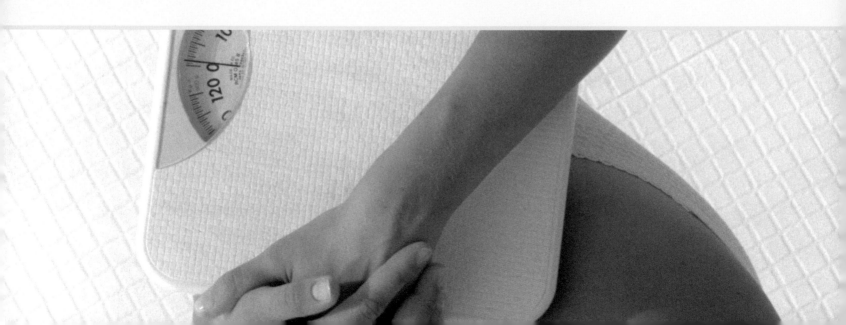

body mass index	18.5–24.9	normal weight
	25.0–29.9	overweight
	30.0–34.9	obesity (level I)
	35.0–39.9	obesity (level II)
	>40	extreme obesity (level III)

The standards for men and women are roughly identical. A BMI of 24.8 means your weight is normal. Figures between 25 and 30 indicate slight overweight. Treatment is only necessary when this is accompanied by diseases. If your BMI is higher than 30, your weight should invariably seek treatment. A BMI larger than 40 generally indicates extreme obesity, which should definitely be treated in order to prevent serious damage of your health.

In the case of older people, these figures can be interpreted somewhat more generously, because our muscle mass decreases as we grow older and the amount of fat tissue increases. This means that a person who maintains a constant weight throughout his life will have more fat tissue at an older age than when he was younger. Research has demonstrated that people over the age of 75 with slight overweight have a longer life expectancy than those with normal weight. It is assumed that the extra weight carries an energy and nutrient store for times of illness.

But what if your BMI is below the above figures? A BMI between 18 and 20 indicates a tendency to underweight. If yours is between 16 and 18, you most certainly are underweight, and if it is lower than 16, you should try to gain a few pounds and possibly seek medical assistance in the interests of your health.

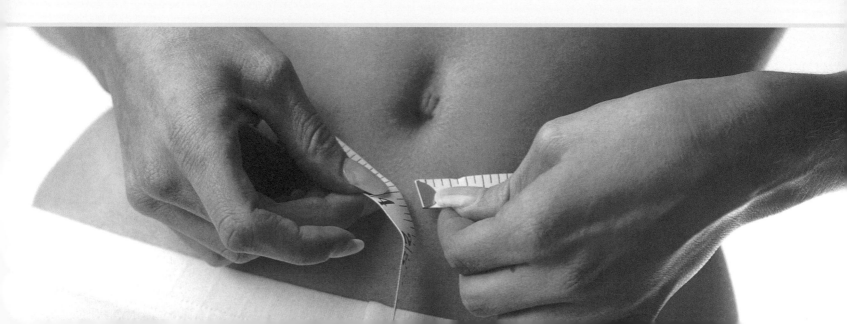

That's why you should make losing weight a long-term project. Set yourself small, readily achievable goals, which will make it easier to keep track of your success. If you change over to a healthier diet and lose about one to two pounds per week, this will have longer lasting effects than any one-sided crash diet. And if every now and then you don't lose weight but in fact gain some, that is no reason to panic. It merely bears out the fact that your body is a living organism that is constantly developing and changing.

Try to get a realistic overview over your eating habits by noting down just how much, what and when you eat for a while. You will not only be able to find out what your preferences (or weaknesses) are, but you'll also be able to determine whether you eat very much or badly in certain situations or at specific times of the day. Then you should try to avoid these traps, for example by replacing your occasional afternoon gâteau with a fruit tart, or by having dried fruit or low-salt crackers instead of crisps while watching television.

Simply trust your instincts when changing your diet. Don't force yourself to eat something you don't like just because it's supposed to be 'oh so healthy'. You will probably find anyway that foods you genuinely dislike don't agree with you.

You can avoid sudden cravings by making sure your blood sugar level remains stable throughout the day. You can do this in quite a number of ways:

- by having nutritious snacks, such as bananas, wholemeal bread, or low-salt crackers. You can read up about these power snacks in the section "How to get rid of bad eating habits".

- by clearly reducing your consumption of alcohol. Never drink alcohol on an empty stomach – it drastically lowers your blood sugar level and sudden cravings for food are the result.

- by reducing the amount of coffee you drink. Caffeine stimulates the release of insulin, and this lowers the blood sugar level.

- by being careful with sugar and largely avoiding sweets. Less is more! Of course, you should treat yourself from time to time, but the chocolate bar shouldn't become a habit.

If you want to lose weight, you should adhere to a simple rule of thumb: don't have more than 60–70 g (about 14 teaspoonfuls) of fat per day, including hidden fats.

- by eating regular meals which supply you with sufficient amounts of carbohydrates and which are rich in nutrients, vitamins and minerals.

The more weight you want to lose, the less fat you should eat. Beware of the many hidden fats contained in sausage, cream and full-fat cheese, sweets, biscuits and nuts. You should only eat these products in small amounts. If you take in about half of your daily fat requirements (approx. 30 g) in spreads, lard or salad oil, you are making an allowance for the hidden fats in food.

You should also drastically reduce your consumption of sugar. According to recommendations of the World Health Organisation (WHO), adults should not have more than 12 teaspoons of sugar a day. This sounds like a lot a t first, but if you look at the list of ingredients on many foods, you will be surprised at how many of them contain sugar. Not only sweets and cake are full of it, but a lot of ready-made savoury meals contain sugar to enhance the flavour.

FASTING: A REJUVENATION CURE FOR BODY AND SOUL

People often fast to reduce weight. Originally, however, fasting was intended to cleanse the body, primarily the stomach and the intestine, from harmful residues. In religious fasting (during the time of Lent leading up to Easter, for example), it was supposed to help you find an inner calm and prepare your soul for tasks to come.

Nowadays, fasting or purification cures are used as forms of therapy, e.g. for chronic disorders of the intestine or as a way of improving your general condition. At first, the intestine is cleansed with bitters and is flushed out. For a limited time, the body is then fed either only water ('natural fasting') or only liquid foods – mostly fresh fruit and vegetable juices ('juice fasting'), or sometimes vegetable broth. The fluid intake should amount to at least four pints per day. After fasting, the body should be given a few days to gradually and carefully get used to firm foods again.

Fasting should not merely be used as a quick method of reducing weight. At first sight it might seem very tempting and simple: you don't have to count calories, there's no need to change to a complicated diet and there

A lot of terms you can find on the list of ingredients on your food products are nothing but aliases for sugar: dextrose, lactose, invert sugar, malt sugar, molasses and honey are frequent pseudonyms for this sweet fattener.

Some Hints on Losing Weight

- Don't skip meals. You'll eat even more at the next meal, and your depleted blood sugar level might make you reach for a chocolate bar.

- Even if it sounds contradictory: eat more often, e.g. have a small, healthy snack between two main meals. This will keep your blood sugar level balanced, your digestive system will be constantly at work burning energy, and your stomach will, in general, get used to smaller portions.

- Drink a lot with your meals: this will fill you up sooner.

- Use a small plate: large plates will tempt you to take too much food, and then you will feel obliged to eat it all up.

- Have small mouthfuls, and chew your food slowly and thoroughly.

- Don't scoop the next bite onto your fork before you have swallowed the last.

- If you want to have a second helping, just wait a moment! It takes your body a bit of time to signal that it is full. The faster you eat, the more you will have eaten before your body tells you it's full.

- Try to avoid the 'housewives' trap': freeze leftovers or use them for the next meal. Don't quickly finish off the leftover potato or gravy on your way into the kitchen.

- Go for a brisk walk after your meal: movement stimulates your digestion, and some extra oxygen will make you feel good.

- Eat one or two apples a day: they are a healthy way of slowing done your appetite, regulating the blood sugar level and lowering your cholesterol levels.

- Experiment! How about Italian or Indian food? Apart from providing you with a lot of low-fat dishes, other countries also add variety to your menu.

Spicy dishes get your metabolism going – for hours. So use chilli powder, mustard or pepper instead of salt.

Plan little 'sins' from the start. Otherwise you will develop such a craving for the forbidden goodies that you will eat a lot of them and end up with a bad conscience. Occasional pleasure without regret is far more sensible.

Get into the habit of writing a shopping list and then sticking to it! Along with "sensible" food, it could contain one or two goodies. Then you won't have the feeling that shopping is a necessary evil and you can look forward to a few treats.

Never go shopping on an empty stomach! You will buy not only more than you need, but also products that contain a lot of fat.

● Don't eat to comfort yourself when you are sad, homesick or frustrated. In such situations, it is better to look for other ways of treating yourself: put some flowers on your desk, have an aromatic soak in the tub, go to the hairdresser, buy a nice T-shirt 'just for fun' – you're bound to think of something.

● Look for support. Tell your family and friends about your goal to lose weight and ask them for moral support. Maybe the usual cream cake won't be served at the next family reunion…

● Don't wait for the diet to show effects before looking after your appearance. Start feeling good about yourself today: go to the hairdresser or buy some new clothes – make sure you maintain a positive attitude. It's a good and healthy thing to be happy with yourself.

Juice fasting is less exhausting for your body than natural fasting, because the fresh juice can ensure your body at least a basic supply of vitamins, minerals and further nutrients.

are immediate results. But the radical reduction of food intake places a strain on your body.

When you are fasting, your body shifts from an 'external' to an 'internal' diet: it starts processing cells and substances from within the body – mostly those that are old or infected. This change, as well as the thorough cleansing taking place while you are fasting, are often accompanied by physical complaints such as nausea, dizziness and headaches.

Before you start fasting for the first time, you should seek medical advice and possibly do it under professional observation. After that, you can supervise your own occasional fasting cures – but only if you are in a healthy condition. If you don't feel completely healthy, you should definitely consult your doctor before fasting.

When carried out sensibly and properly, fasting cures can be very good for your organism. The simultaneous processes of purification and detoxification cleanse your body and get rid of damaging residues as well as mobilising the body's inherent healing abilities. Fasting is supposed to have highly beneficial effects in cases of skin diseases, allergies, nervous and psychological problems, disorders of the metabolism and cardiovascular system, rheumatism, and illnesses affecting the respiratory tract or the digestive system.

Some people experience so-called 'fasting euphoria' during their fasting cure – a feeling of elation, ease and increased sensitivity. There are frequent reports of an energy boost, which in part probably stems from the fact that the energy otherwise needed to digest foods is made additionally available.

If possible, fasting should be an integral process. It makes sense to give your entire body and soul a relaxing break while fasting. Regular breaks and long sleeping hours do only help your organism to deal with the reduced food intake, but they should also be regarded as an opportunity to relax – to literally give yourself some peace and (inner) quiet. It is important that the inner cleansing process is accompanied by regular mouth and skin care.

You should try to switch off outward sources of stress. Some books on fasting advise you to dispense with television, radio and newspapers in order to avoid negative impressions and to keep social contacts to a minimum,

Spring and autumn – the seasons in which nature's juices come and go – are the best times for fasting.

so that you can focus exclusively on yourself. It is, of course, up to you how many of these recommendations you apply and to what extent.

Fasting should not be a means of self-castigation, but rather of improving your general condition. Should you lose weight rapidly, have sudden, intense hunger pangs, feel extremely dizzy, weak or nervous, then you should stop fasting. It should not turn into a starvation diet (for reasons of health), because starving your body leads to under-nourishment and can have serious side-effects.

How to Combat Cellulitis

Practically all women sooner or later battle with the unsightly dents that mostly show up on their bottom and thighs. An unbalanced diet low in fibre promotes this feared condition. If the waste products remain in your intestine for an excessive amount of time, your sensitive metabolism will be disrupted. This leads to constipation, which stops the blood circulation from working properly. The blood and lymph vessels in your pelvis are strained. The more difficult it is for the blood to flow through your body, the weaker the blood renewal in the affected body part. Water and metabolic waste products are retained in the tissues and support the development of cellulitis.

Fibrous and low-fat foods are recommended to prevent this. In addition, you should drink a lot of water and unsweetened herbal or fruit teas – that will get your metabolism going and has a purifying effect. You should eat a lot of raw fruit and vegetables, wholemeal products as well as lean meat and skimmed milk products. Pure fruit and vegetable juices are suitable, as are mineral water and herbal teas. You should avoid extremely salty or sugary foods, those with a high fat content, foods made with refined products or containing starch, along with fatty meat, fast food, lemonade and alcoholic beverages.

Regular physical activity is the be-all and end-all for smooth, firm thighs. A change of diet is useful but on its own not sufficient to prevent and fight cellulitis.

STAYING FIT AND SUPPLE WITH ADVANCING AGE

A lot of people aren't satisfied with their figure. Dieting seems to be the only solution, but positive results are seldom to be seen. Fitness training means turning exercise into a habit. Today, most people suffer from a lack of exercise. We no longer walk up the stairs anymore, because the lift is faster and more convenient. We use our cars for the shortest trips just to save ourselves from walking a few steps. We are always in a hurry with one appointment after another in our business activities as well as our private lives. The consequences of such a lifestyle are that our bodies slowly but surely begin to lose their suppleness, physical endurance and muscular strength. This means that your figure will suffer – and even worse, your general well-being deteriorates and you start to lose your enjoyment of life. You feel thoroughly unwell, without being ill. In fact, however, it is not difficult to get fit again – but you have to understand that the solution lies in regular exercise.

FITNESS BEGINS IN YOUR HEAD

If you already exercise regularly, go jogging or swimming frequently, go to a fitness centre or are an active member of a sports club, it is possible that you will not find this chapter particularly relevant or interesting – unless of course you would like to find out about some new or additional training methods.

Yet if you number among those people who can only vaguely remember gymnastics and sports from your school days, you should read the following pages attentively and without prejudice. And one more thing: try to be honest with yourself. There's no point in telling yourself that you get enough exercise every day – in the hectic office environment, behind a counter or at home – and that you therefore don't need any additional exercise or other physical activity. That is only an excuse, for this kind of exercise neither fills your lungs with oxygen nor does it strengthen your cardiovascular system. This treadmill of daily life only makes you feel tired, exhausted and ill.

You are quite likely to be satisfied with the amount of exercise you get every day if you are satisfied with your image in the mirror, maybe even in a bathing suit or underwear. You might even feel perfectly well, both physically and emotionally. If this is the case, then it is not very likely that anything will convince you to finally give your body some systematic exercise. For as long as everything is fine and the machine known as the 'human body' is functioning properly, very few people are astute enough to see the need to do something for the regeneration and preservation of this efficiency. Especially while we are still young it can be very tempting to be careless with our energy in order to meet the demands of today's business world.

On the other hand, perhaps you number among those people who sometimes are more than a little unsatisfied with the flab to be found here and there or the pot belly they can no longer hide. And maybe you are beginning to feel rather uncomfortable about obviously not being in as quite a good shape as used to be: you get tired faster, often feel listless and exhausted. As soon as you no longer play down these insights and blame them on your progressing age, but accept the fact that the cause lies in your monotonous life style, then you are already on the way to improvement.

Generally, people who have never exercised at all are only willing to change their lifestyle once their body shows the first signs of no longer being able to cope with such neglect. At this point, however, it becomes more difficult to regain your former efficiency. Start giving your body now what it desperately needs: exercise, exercise and even more exercise!

An Honest Assessment

Very rarely in daily life – regardless of whether the rut of your job or the tiring monotony of leading a household is consuming you – will you have the nerve to spend any considerable length of time by yourself. When appointments are breathing down your neck and dominating your life, you will generally consider the question of whether your body is lacking exercise a somewhat irrelevant one. A lot of people consider the pace of everyday life to be sufficient in the way of daily exercise. And some people might even think you were pulling their leg if they were to be faced with the demand of doing more physical exercise. There are more important responsibilities than exercising the body. A widely accepted assumption is that only people who are primarily concerned with their looks and don't have to or don't want to take their work or their responsibilities at home seriously have the time for exercising or in fact show any interest in it at all.

This, however, is fundamentally wrong, for by deliberately going without the physical exercise that is in no way related to the daily rush in your job, you are systematically reducing your body's efficiency. Sooner or later, it will leave you in the lurch. Women tend to notice this sooner because they begin to dislike their appearance at some point in time. Men, on the other hand, tend to care less about their looks: they are confronted with the truth at the latest when they are troubled by some small, yet annoying complaint.

Take a couple of hours to think about your life, maybe over a good cup of tea. You could also write down what you are thinking about. Review your daily life: write down the course of an average day in your life. Then ask yourself whether there might not be a bit of time here or there in which you can relax and catch your breath. When you drop into bed in the evenings – do you feel pleasantly tired? Or are you so exhausted that you just drop off to sleep? Or do you literally have to fight for sleep because so many worries are still on your mind?

What about your spare time? Do you just hang around? Do you usually end up in a restaurant? Do you always sit around with friends? Or do you work around the house or in your garden? If the weather is fine, would you pack a bag and just go out walking for a day? When was the last time you went to the swimming pool – or did some exercises in front of an open window at the weekend?

It would be nice if – at the end of your contemplation – you realised that up to now you have been more or less neglecting your body and have been largely ignoring its legitimate rights. This insight will enable you to radically change your life from one day to the next, yet without a lot of effort or renunciations.

SETTING YOUR OWN PERSONAL GOALS

Everybody needs physical exercise. Yet, individual needs cannot be generalised. We need specifically tailored exercise routines to meet our own lack of exercise.

A lot of people have reached the same stage as you have, in other words they desire to finally do something – yet they fail even despite their good resolutions. It is very much like a diet that you dive into from one day to the next in order to lose a lot of weight. Because there's no fun in it, you eventually find thousands of reasons for abandoning your diet sooner than you should and postponing it to a later date. Should you now suddenly decide you want to exercise and immediately pay a year's membership for your health centre, you might run the risk of not going through with your ambitious plans. Lots of people have joined fitness centres and then even showed up there a few times – and that then was the end of it. We all know the reasons: you haven't got the time; it's not your thing after all; it's no fun.

You need to make a realistic plan. Your goals should be moderate ones and the self-prescribed fitness therapy should be fun. And what is most important, you should be able to see real results as soon as possible: you should really lose a few pounds, start feeling better and enjoy your physical activities.

If you approach your fitness training programme in much the same way as you would approach an appointment at the dentist's – you have to go, but don't really want to – then you've already lost the battle right from the beginning. In such a case, it will only be a matter of time until you unceremoneously do away with your good intentions. So regardless of what kind of physical exercise you engage in, you should become addicted to it. Then you will be successful and your renewed fitness will be guaranteed. In other words, you will soon be quite surprised and fascinated by the renewed energy you have found. After all, it is not particularly difficult to regain a state of physical fitness, and it doesn't even take a lot of time to do so. All you have to do is to go about it properly and persevere.

If you want a youthful figure, you will of course have to work for it! However, be sure to set yourself realistic goals, otherwise you may well be tempted to give up too easily.

You will not succeed without a goal. A good goal will give you the energy you need. You have to set this goal yourself. Maybe you would finally like to wear a fancy bikini again this summer – something you haven't dared for a while because you were starting to feel ashamed of your body. Or you would like to wear one of your old favourites that is rather clingy and hasn't fit you properly for some time to a special occasion? Maybe you no longer want to feel exhausted in the evenings, always having to disappoint your partner who would still like to take you out to dinner? You might want to prove to a friend or acquaintance that you can get rid of your flab after all. And if you do not want to succumb to your inner voice tempting you to skip just this one scheduled training session, then all you have to do is to remember your goal – a realistic, powerful goal will give you the strength to overcome your laziness and do your exercises or go to the fitness centre.

Don't Overdo it!

Begin gently; don't overdo it. If you haven't exercised at all up to now then you shouldn't attempt anything marathon-like. Begin with simple exercises. If you think you can spend five minutes on exercising every day, that's fantastic. It's quite sufficient even to exercise three times a week for fifteen minutes each, but make sure you schedule these times and adhere to them. Make up your own personal exercise routine from the exercises described later in this chapter. Make sure it is varied and if you don't like a certain exercise, then it is better to go without it.

A defined goal also needs a specified time frame. Allow yourself four weeks. If you make thorough use of this period of time, you will already see some progress after four weeks: the exercises will seem simpler, you won't get out of breath as quickly as you used to, you might even feel like adding some exercises to your routine every now and then or even have a desire to extend your sessions by a few minutes. In fact, you might even want to exercise on an additional day. And when you step on the scales, you will see what progress you have been making. In parallel to exercising you should of course make sure that your diet is well-balanced, for exercise and nutrition supplement each other.

Once you have reached your first goal, everything will become a lot easier from then on. You will set yourself another goal: maybe you want to lose a certain amount of weight, want to become more supple, more

It is quite normal for exercise to get you going and to increase your breathing rate. Yet you shouldn't, of course, exercise so vigorously that you have to gasp for breath.

balanced emotionally or more active. Make yourself consciously aware of the fact that you are feeling much better in general – that you feel more efficient; that your old tiredness is waning and that you feel as strong as a horse.

ACCEPT YOUR LIMITS

If you are completely healthy, there is no need to consult a physician before beginning to exercise. Yet, you should get a doctor to examine you and discuss the extent of your training with him or her if you suffer from some disorder or other, such as diabetes, epileptic fits, chronic back-ache, joint problems, heart and circulation illnesses, as well as after a heart attack or stroke, or if you are seriously overweight. If you even want to become intensively involved in physical exercise, e.g. in a sports club or fitness centre, are over forty and haven't exercised a lot up to now, you should also consult a doctor. A gentle approach with simple exercises will certainly not damage your health. The only cause for concern is if you go beyond your goal and overdo it.

Reputable fitness centres generally work together with a sports doctor, who will examine you before you begin training and who will advise you throughout. It would not be advisable to simply sit down at the equipment and start. Only young people in good physical condition can do this.

Even if you have had a heart attack, for example, physical exercise is in no way taboo for you. On the contrary: specific exercises can increase the performance of your heart after an attack. And conscious exercise will help prevent high blood pressure, the greatest risk factor for a further heart attack. Yet, you should only do this under medical observation. It is also important that you don't overstrain yourself: strain is allowed and even desired, for it is good for a normal, healthy body to be challenged. A weakened organism can also be challenged, yet individual limits must be more closely observed than in a healthy person.

If you are over thirty-five, haven't exercised for a long time, or suffer from specific health risks, it is essential that you consult a doctor before beginning to exercise.

People suffering from osteoporosis often fear exercising because they think they might fracture their bones by clumsy movements. That is wrong, because most fractures occur in normal, everyday movements, e.g. when lifting a heavy object the wrong way. In your work-out, you should then practise doing such everyday movements – e.g. bending and lifting objects – correctly. Flexibility exercises won't heal osteoporosis, but have

positive effects on its progression. Proper movements support the bone structure because movement helps to store increased amounts of calcium in the bones and thereby strengthens them. If you begin exercising regularly at an early age, you might even be able to completely avoid getting osteoporosis later.

Before and after each training session, you should check your heart rate. Put two fingers on the artery in your wrist and count your pulse rate for 15 seconds. Multiply the result by four and you have your heart rate per minute. A maximum heart rate after exercising should be 130 to 160 beats per minute in 20 to 30-year-olds, 120 to 150 beats per minute in 30 to 40-year-olds, and 116 to 144 in 40 to 50-year-olds. If in doubt, you can ask your doctor to determine your personal maximum. Ideally he should carry out an ECG when your body is resting and when it is exercising; from this your individual limits can be deduced.

There are also a number of electronic devices available which can be worn like a watch and constantly show your pulse while exercising. Since your pulse is an ideal indicator of controlling your performance, such a device is certainly useful because it can show you exactly how each phase of your work-out is affecting your body. It shows you how much you can exercise and when you have reached your limits. However, such a device is only useful once you have moved beyond the initial stages of exercising and now want to improve your fitness systematically with other sports such as cycling, running, or using other equipment.

LESS EFFORT IN THE FITNESS CENTRE

A lot of people have difficulties working out on their own. It is simply more fun to do so with a friend or in a group. In addition, you can motivate each other and carry each other along. If you don't really feel like exercising one day and can't be bothered to do your workout, it is much easier to postpone the whole affair if you are on your own. (And quite frequently, you will keep postponing your workout until this becomes a habit that is hard to break.) In a group, there is a certain amount of competition and the members keep a check on each other. Everybody is constantly comparing their own performance with that of the others, even though they might not be consciously aware of it. You don't want to embarrass yourself and will try to informally be accepted by the others if you are just as good or even better. And if you really can't make it for once, you need to come up with a plausible excuse. It even becomes difficult to completely give up the workout because you have taken to the group. In this case, it is no longer merely a workout, but a social experience and contact.

On the other hand, if you join a fitness centre on your own and unfortunately don't manage to make friends or establish contact with a group of like-minded people, you will then be more at risk of giving up. In this case, you won't feel quite so bad about having spent an expensive membership fee in vain.

Finding a fitness centre doesn't seem to be a problem. The fashionable trend of staying healthy, fit and beautiful has caused several such centres to open. Yet, it is all the more difficult to find one you can trust. Make absolutely sure whether you are dealing with a body-building centre or a fitness centre. The name won't necessarily indicate the subtle difference. Body-building centres offer very one-sided workouts, which is why they are not suitable. But some fitness centres with attractive names should also not be trusted too naively.

Once you have found a suitable place, go there and take a close and critical look at it. What does the place look like? Is there enough equipment to exercise your stamina, i.e. are there enough stationary bikes, step masters, and treadmills? Is there specific equipment for back and stomach training? Such equipment is absolutely essential for you. On the other hand, vigorous weight training is not a good idea. Let someone show you the range of exercises on offer. Do these include daily aerobics courses? Are there specific exercise courses?

In your first consultation you should be offered a test, because otherwise the trainer will have no possibility of tailoring a training programme specifically to your physical status and personal goals. There is no sense in just going into the centre whenever you feel like it and exercising with this or that equipment on a whim – this can even be dangerous. This is the reason why the manager of the centre and if possible all other staff members should have had specific training. Ask for their references. It is also not a good sign if there is hardly any staff around the place. One trainer cannot attend to all equipment equally well at the same time. Some centres even co-operate with a sports doctor who does the entry test and designs your own individual training programme.

You should only agree to a prolonged period of membership if you have examined the whole place thoroughly and carefully considered your decision. You definitely shouldn't sign any contracts or agreements on your first visit anyway. And even better: try to arrange a practice session. Reputable centres mostly offer this in any case, in order to win over potential customers.

THE ALTERNATIVE: SPORTS CLUBS

Fitness centres are the modern version of the good old sports club. You should also consider whether there is a sports club near you that offers aerobic courses, ball games or athletics, maybe even specifically for women. Becoming a member of a club has a few advantages over a purely commercial fitness centre. Often the atmosphere in a sports club isn't quite as trendy, but the staff and members normally know what they are on about. Professional and competent guidance is basically guaranteed in a sports club. In addition, you can normally make friends more quickly in such clubs because sports clubs not only take their sport very seriously but also endeavour to bring their members together to form a close-knit group. To do so they offer a variety of social activities such as Christmas functions, dance evenings, organised trips, picknicks and hikes. You should also bear in mind that membership in a sports club tends to be cheaper than in a fitness centre.

And now for a few comments on your outfit. In fitness centres most people wear trendy leotards, the design of which rarely has anything to do with the demands of their training. If you really like wearing trendy clothes, do so by all means. However, because leotards tend to be very clingy, they also show every blemish in your figure, which a lot of women don't like about them. It can look very sexy on a twenty-year-old who is in good shape. But once your proportions no longer look perfect due to your advanced age, such an outfit could look silly. That's why you should wear what you want and what might even hide the flab you want to get rid of by exercising. Your clothes can be loose-fitting. The only condition is that they should not hinder you, are comfortable and allow your body to breathe. The same applies to your feet: wear light trainers or woollen socks.

Basically, it does not matter what type of physical exercise you decide on. The important thing is that you enjoy it – this is the best way of ensuring that you will engage in regular exercise.

WARMING UP

Any kind of physical exercise should be preceded by a brief warm-up phase. Whether you are doing aerobics, running or going for a swim, you can't force your body to give maximum performance from a resting state from one minute to the next. To warm up your muscles you can of course briskly go up and down the stairs for five minutes. Yet it is much more practical to do a few standard warm-up exercises.

For the first exercise, stand upright, with your legs slightly apart. Your arms and shoulders should be relaxed (1). This exercise is not very spectacular, but very effective: simply move up your shoulders from this relaxed starting position (2).

A variant of this warm-up exercise: lift your shoulders as far as possible from the starting position (3), and then roll them backwards, pressing your shoulder blades together (4). Then return to the starting position. Repeat this exercise about 10 times.

You should stop exercising as soon as you feel pain; and you should do the same should you start feeling dizzy. You have probably overdone it or are going down with a cold. When you are suffering from an infection, with or without a temperature, you should never overtax your body by exercising. Should you feel un-pleasantly exhausted after a training session, you should do less in the next session. If your symptoms don't improve, consult a doctor about the possible causes.

Another warm-up exercise: for the starting position, stand with your legs slightly apart with your torso slightly leaning forward. It is essential to keep your chest and back very straight (1).

Now, shift the weight to your left leg and bend it, leaving your right leg fully stretched out. Both feet should remain firmly on the ground. You can feel the inside of your right thigh being stretched (2). Try to stay in this position for five seconds. Repeat five times, then repeat this exercise with the other leg (3).

Here are a series of exercises that you can do from the same starting position as the previous ones. Let your head sink forward; your chin should nearly rest on your chest (4). Then lift your head and stretch your neck (5). Repeat five times.

In the second stage, allow your head to fall to one side. Your shoulders should remain lowered (6).Then lift your head back into the centre and stretch your neck while doing so. Then do the same with the other side (7). Repeat this exercise five times.

As a third stage of this exercise, turn your head to one side as if you were trying to look over your shoulder (8). Then look straight ahead again and lift your shoulders. Now do the same with the other side (9) and repeat the whole stage about five times.

How to Effectively Supplement Your Exercise

Regular exercise primarily strengthens your muscles and tones certain parts of your body. It also helps to regain your former suppleness. However, your body wants to be challenged from head to toe. This is why you should supplement your exercises by aerobic training to increase your stamina. Don't let this term intimidate you – it is not our intention to turn you into a top athlete.

Aerobic training is suitable for just about everybody and in fact indispensable to anyone whose exercise programme would otherwise be one-sided.

The term 'aerobic' simply means 'dependent on oxygen'. Your organism requires sufficient oxygen for its muscles to work properly. In aerobic metabolism, your body requires oxygen to break down glycogen and fatty acids. If you strain your body beyond its capacity, it has no additional oxygen for this metabolism and will start producing the additional energy needed without the aid of oxygen. This is known as anaerobic metabolism (independent of oxygen), an emergency process which creates an excess of lactic acid and other substances in the muscles; this is why your muscles become sore after a lengthy exercise session. The negative effect of this waste product is that the function of your muscles is limited and performance drastically reduced. In other words: if you are not aware of your physical limits and adhere to them, you will quickly find yourself defeated because your muscles will stop working as you want them to.

Your body is able to adapt quickly to certain demands in performance. If you train regularly and in the right way – e.g. by jogging, swimming, walking or cycling – your body will soon become accustomed to the increased strain. By this means, you can gradually but constantly challenge your body to higher performance.

In this way you can systematically increase the limits of your physical performance, and this will in turn have highly beneficial effects on your organism: for example, you will lower your heart rate. This means you will not get out of breath after only the slightest physical exertion. You will easily be able to run up the stairs – something you would have almost considered an impossibility not long ago. Your body will thus become more efficient, not in order to win medals, but to make your life easier and more pleasant for you. For you will feel much better, and stressful situations will no longer upset you so often. In addition, physical exercise releases endorphins, which stimulate you and encourage a general feeling of well-being.

ANAEROBIC EXERCISES

Some kinds of exercise are also very suitable for training your stamina. However, such exercises significantly differ from those presented in this chapter. Aerobics involve vigorous body movements to the beat of fast music. Your body breaks down a lot of fat. If you want to lose weight, aerobics classes are very suitable for you. Also, a lot of people enjoy exercising to popular music in a group.

BALL GAMES AND DANCING

Whether it be football, volleyball, squash, tennis or badminton, these games all demand a lot of quick movement and are therefore classed as aerobic sports. Apart from an increased breakdown of fat, they increase your flexibility and dexterity.

Of course, another important advantage of any team sport is that the competitive atmosphere often allows you to forget that you are exercising at all. Some people find repeating the same exercises over and over again rather boring. In ball games you quickly forget that you are exercising – you just want to win.

Even though golf might not seem to be a very strenuous kind of sport, it should not be underestimated. Wielding with the golf clubs is excellent exercise for your shoulders, arms and legs. In addition, a golfer has to walk quite a number of miles per game.

Although step dancing is not a ball game, it also numbers among the aerobic sports that train the body's general stamina as well as your buttocks, thighs and calves.

Belly dancing is also often considered a good type of sport. Surely, this specific way of dancing is demanding and trains your stamina; it exercises certain groups of muscles as well as being a lot of fun. Yet, this applies to dancing in general whether you do it as a sport or in your leisure time. If

you watch a good rock 'n' roll group, you will realise that you are watching top-class sportspeople. But even waltzing for an hour or any other kind of dancing will not only make you perspire but can possibly give you very sore muscles the following day. Regardless, dancing releases a lot of energy by burning up calories.

JOGGING AND WALKING

Jogging also uses up a lot of energy and is an uncomplicated type of sport that provides you with fantastic stamina training. Jogging strengthens the muscles of your legs, but your entire cardiovascular system will also profit from this type of exercise.

If you want to take up jogging, you shouldn't just start straight away. Even though this sport looks incredibly harmless, jogging is very demanding on your body. Be sure to consult your doctor if you haven't been very active until now or have taken a long break from exercising.

You don't need a lot of equipment for jogging, but there are a few very important things to keep in mind. For example, you need suitable shoes. You should also not forget that your body temperature rises to about 39 °C (102 °F) after a few minutes and that your body loses a significant amount of liquid through perspiration. You should consider this in your choice of clothing: it must conduct the excess heat to the outside. Make sure to drink a lot afterwards (or in between when running long distances) to compensate for the loss of water through sweating.

You should never go jogging without doing some warm-up exercises beforehand. Your metabolism needs to be stimulated and the blood vessels of your skeletal muscles need to be dilated. There is, by the way, no point in warming your muscles externally, e.g. by means of warm clothing or heat. Your muscles need to be warmed up actively. Also, make sure you do not abruptly end your training session: simply run more slowly for the last stretch and finish by walking. Finally, you should do some simple stretching exercises to end your workout. Your muscles need to be gradually returned to a resting state.

The less performance-oriented variety of jogging is walking – 'power walking', not your leisurely Sunday afternoon stroll. It does not strain your body as much as jogging does and that's why it is highly suitable for anyone who

If you exercise vigorously and lose a lot of fluid through perspiring, you need to make sure that you replace this quickly. If you are going on an extended cycling or running tour, it is essential that you drink something in between.

does not feel confident enough to go jogging. The difference between walking and running lies in the way in which your feet are used. Whereas in running, you sometimes seem to be flying over the ground with neither foot touching it for the briefest of moments, in walking, one foot is always firmly in contact with the ground. Your arms swing along in the rhythm of walking and you should be looking straight ahead. Power walking can be compared to very brisk hiking, which also differs from your leisurely 'walk' by its regularity of movement and the persistent forward movement.

Biking

If you possess the appropriate bike and clothing (including gloves, shoes and helmet) and feel safe on your bike, then you can slowly begin to train. It is also important though to not overdo it at the beginning, but to start slowly and according to a schedule that takes your specific needs into consideration.

Fitness in Water

Swimming is generally considered to be the type of sport that is best suited to your body and that exercises it the most effectively. This is partly due to the fact that gravity is largely neutralised in water, so that your body weight is reduced by 90%. As a result, only a minimum of strain is placed on your joints.

There are various swimming techniques. Backstroke is especially suitable, because your chest muscles are stretched by the alternating arm movements. Apart from movement, the experience of water as an element plays an important role that should not be underestimated. For water strengthens and harmonises body and soul. If the pool is fed by mineral springs you will also profit from the beneficial effects on your health.

The leisure industry has come up with a variety of implements and gadgets that are sold in connection with the term 'aqua fitness'. For example, you can get pontoons that you attach to your feet, which are supposed to enable you to walk in the water. If you enjoy such things, go ahead and use them; on the other hand, they are not necessary for sensible training. They provide more of a seasonal entertainment. Such gadgets cannot replace your own activity.

Avoid running or walking where there are no paths – there is too much danger of tripping and injuring yourself. Sand and gravel are also unsuitable for this kind of sport. Running stimulates your breathing: that's why you should avoid running in industrial areas or near major roads. The increased intake of carbon monoxide produced by factories and traffic is anything but healthy.

PROBLEM ZONE: THIGHS

Every woman has her own problem zones. These critical areas can be the stomach, hips, thighs or buttocks, for example. 'Problem' means that too much fat has accumulated in this particular area – and that doesn't look very attractive. Diets won't help at all because these areas of fat are very stubborn. Yet, you can deal with them with specific and consistent exercise (as well as by adapting your diet).

The various exercises focus on certain groups of muscles. That's why you need to choose those exercises that tackle your problem zones. You shouldn't be too concerned with this however, since most women have more then just one problem zone. Maybe you not only have big thighs,

but also a flabby tummy, and perhaps you're not quite satisfied with your bottom either. Put your own exercise programme together according to your needs. You don't have to stick to the same routine every time either. Vary it, for all the muscles of your body can do with some exercise, even though some may need it more than others.

The first exercise, which is intended to firm your thighs, is quite simple. (But before you begin, you should always do five minutes of warm-up exercises!) Lie down on your back comfortably (1), then spread out your arms horizontally to the side and pull up your knees towards your chest (2). Put a ball or small cushion between your knees and press them together ten to fifteen times in a slow rhythm (3).

And now it is time for the second exercise. Lie on your back with your legs stretched out and push your backbone into the mat. Your arms are at your sides with your palms facing downwards; spread them away from your body again, bend your legs and pull up your knees towards your chest. Keep your legs together and then stretch them straight into the air (4). Move your legs as far apart as you can and then bring them together again (5). Repeat this five times. Then return to the starting position, stay like this for a few minutes and relax.

PROBLEM ZONE: BOTTOM

The shape of your bottom is largely determined by three muscles: the gluteus maximus, the gluteus medius and the gluteus minimus. The size of your bottom, however, is determined by the fatty tissue; and fat can be exercised away, leaving you with a nice firm bottom. Every kind of movement, regardless of whether you take the stairs, go jogging or cycling, will help you to make a large bottom more attractive. And of course, there are specific exercises to help you.

For the first exercise, lie down with your legs slightly apart, and then bend them (1). Your arms should lie at the side of your body, with your palms facing down. Slowly lift up your bottom and shift the weight to your back and shoulders. Leave your feet on the ground; your arms remain in position. When you have lifted your bottom, tense its muscles several times (2). Then lower your bottom to the ground again and start over again. You will find this little exercise quite exhausting at first, and you will have had enough after about five repeats. Try to increase the number of repeats every time you exercise.

Here is another exercise for your bottom with the same starting position as the previous exercise (3). After bending your legs, put the outside of your left foot onto your right knee. At the same time push your right knee outwards a little (4). Finally, take hold of your right thigh with both hands and slowly pull the leg towards your chest (5). This exercise needs to be carried out very slowly and with concentration. Do the exercise with the other leg and repeat the whole set four times.

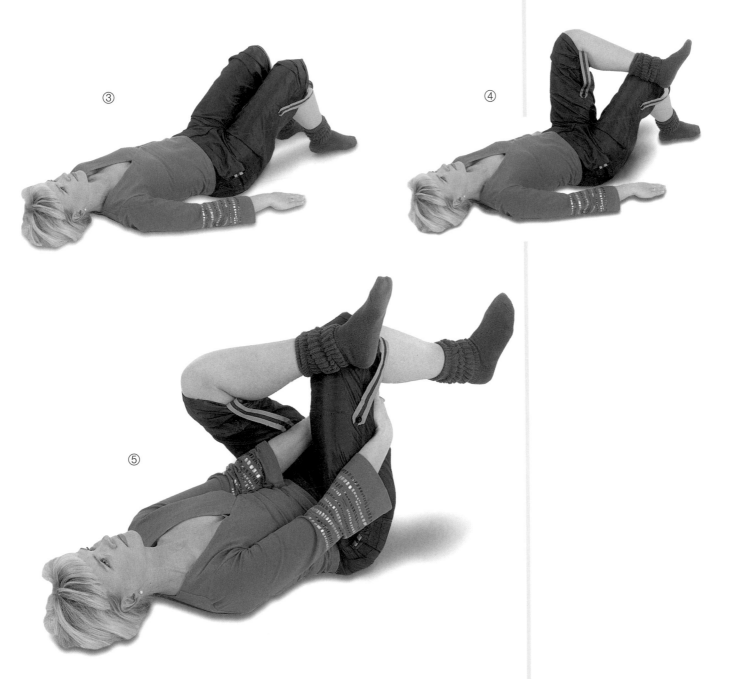

③

④

⑤

PROBLEM ZONE: TUMMY

Once their stomach muscles start to slacken, a lot of women start to think whistfully back to their younger years, when they could wear a bikini. Unfortunately, a flabby tummy has two causes: overweight and lack of exercise. Specific exercises are useful, but they are not the only cure. You will also have to lose weight.

At first you should develop a feeling for your stomach muscles. This can be done by a very simple exercise. Lie on your back, with your legs bent and your arms at your sides, palms facing downwards (1). Then push your lower spine towards the ground by using your stomach muscles (2). Hold this position for a few seconds. You should clearly feel tension in your stomach muscles. Then relax these muscles again. Repeat several times and make sure you do this exercise very slowly.

A second exercise with the same starting position: slowly lift your head and try to keep the tension in your stomach muscles, leaving your legs and arms as they are (3).

You can increase the difficulty with another version of this exercise. Keep the same starting position as in the previous exercises for a firmer tummy. Slowly lift your calves until they are parallel to the floor (4). Keep them in this position. Now put your hands under your head and curl up your spine until your head is lifted off the ground (5).

To further increase the level, do the following exercise: try to move your shoulder towards the diagonally opposite hip (6). This slight twist can be repeated several times in both directions. Because this exercise is very tiring, you should stop when it starts to get too difficult. However, try to increase the number of times you repeat this exercise with every workout.

④

⑤

⑥

PROBLEM ZONE: BUST

Your breasts do not possess any muscles, but are only supported by tendons. If you do not support your bust with a bra, it will simply abide by the laws of gravity. This problem increases with the size of your bust. Once it has slackened, there is nothing you can do about it even with muscle training. Specific exercises, however, can strengthen the muscles under your arms which can support your bust a little.

For the first exercise, stand upright, with your head straight, your chin forward, your legs slightly apart and your arms at your sides (1). Bring your hands together behind your back and then slowly lift your arms without changing your posture, i.e. without leaning forwards (2).

From the same starting position, lift your arms until they are horizontal (3). Describe five to ten small circular movements with both arms at the same time – first forwards, then backwards.

For the third exercise, assume the same starting position. Cross one arm over the other and then stretch them as far forwards as you can (4). Then lift your outstretched arms above your head (5).

For the fourth exercise go down onto your hands and knees. Your weight is carried by your outstretched arms and your knees (6). Gradually lower your body and then push it up again (7). Try repeating this five times. If you are able to, you can perhaps repeat this exercise up to twenty times. You can also cross your feet, which will give you a bit more balance.

PROBLEM ZONE: BACK

Backache is a serious problem, which is why you should always include a back-strengthening exercise in your training programme even if you are lucky enough to not have been plagued by back problems so far. You should generally attempt to avoid extreme inward curving of your lower spine with all of these exercises.

For the first exercise, you should lie down on your stomach. Stretch both arms above your head and place them on the floor (1). Now tense your stomach muscles and lift your outstretched arms with the palms of your hands facing each other (2).

For the second exercise, you need to slightly change the starting position: put a cushion or a rolled-up towel under your stomach (3). Make sure you are still lying comfortably. Now bend your legs and lift them a little (4). Try to hold the tension briefly. Put your legs back onto the ground, pause for a short time and repeat another four times.

For the third exercise, sit on your heels. Press your chest onto your thighs, with your arms on the floor above your head (5). Now slowly lift your torso and try to keep your arms stretched horizontally (6).

The fourth exercise is more complicated. Lie down on the floor and pull one leg up at the side of your body. Your arms are stretched out on the floor above your head (7). Now push one arm into the floor and lift the other up, keeping it stretched out (8). Now lift both arms simultaneously until they are about level with your shoulders (9). You might even be able to do this version: place your hands behind your neck and lift your elbows (10). During all these exercises you should be looking at the floor.

PROBLEM: POSTURE

Whenever you exercise the muscles supporting your pelvis and torso, you are also doing something for your posture. The starting position for the first exercise: lie on your side, stretch the arm lying on the floor above your head and support your torso with the other arm (1). Now lift the upper leg as far up as possible (2).

You need a certain amount of balance for the second exercise. Sit on the floor and bend your legs. Lean backwards onto your arms, with your elbows bent slightly. You hands should form a fist (3). Now slowly lift your pelvis until your torso and thighs form a fairly straight line (4).

For the third exercise, lie on your back again with your legs bent and your hands next to your bottom with the palms facing downwards (5). Lift your pelvis until your torso and thighs form a straight line (6). In this position, pull your toes towards your legs (7). Then stretch one leg upwards, with your toes still pulled forward. Your torso, thighs and lower leg should form a nice straight line (8).

PROBLEM ZONE: NECK

By regularly exercising your neck muscles, you can prevent them from tensing up due to the strain of your job and can even help to relieve tension in this area. These are very simple exercises that should be done slowly and without a lot of effort.

For the first exercise, sit down on a chair comfortably with your back straight. Put one hand on your head (1) and gently pull your head to the side. Now try pushing your hand aside and your head back to the starting position. Maintain this tension for a few seconds (2).

The second exercise will help you to stretch the muscles in your neck: sit on a chair and fold your hands behind your neck (3). Now pull your head forwards with your hands still folded (4).

Exercise number three is a version in which you sit on the floor with your legs bent. Sit up straight and put your hands on the back of your head (5) and pull it towards your knees (6). To do this, you will round your back and lower your pelvis. Make sure that the tension isn't too strong.

EXERCISING WITH THE PHYSIOTHERAPY BALL

It is a lot of fun to work out with a large physiotherapy ball, and you can use it in a lot of exercises.

The starting position for exercise number one: lie on your back with your legs bent; the ball is on your stomach and your hands are holding it (1). Now roll the ball up to your knees and simultaneously lift your head and shoulders from the ground (2). Remain in this position for a short time and then roll the ball back again. Repeat this about ten times. You can alter the exercise by only rolling the ball up one leg – this will strengthen the diagonal stomach muscles (3).

If you tend to get backache when working at a desk, you should try to exchange your chair for a large physiotherapy ball. You will then sit much more comfortably and with a healthier posture.

Exercise number two will strengthen the stomach muscles. Sit on the ball with your legs slightly apart. Move your chest forward (4). Now slowly move your feet forward so that the ball rolls into the small of your back. Try keeping your torso as straight as possible. Now lift up your outstretched arms (5). Don't do this exercise on a slippery floor, otherwise the ball could roll away from beneath you.

④

⑤

EXERCISING WITH THE PHYSIOTHERAPY BALL

The third exercise can be a lot of fun. But watch out that you don't break anything when throwing the ball into the air, especially if you are exercising at home. Lie on your back with your legs bent and your feet apart. Hold the ball in front of your chest (1). Throw it up and catch it with your legs (2). Then throw it back to your hands with your legs. Repeat this game ten times.

The fourth exercise is fairly difficult and also demands some dexterity: Lie down on your side, with your upper arm supporting your body and your legs stretched out. The ball is between your legs. Now you should try lifting up the ball from your pelvis. Hold it in this position for a few seconds (3), then turn over and try on the other side.

①

②

③

Exercise five: lie down on the ball on your stomach as relaxed as possible. Let your head hang down. Enjoy this slight stretching for about half a minute. If you want to, you can move the ball around a little (4).

Exercise number five can be done at any time, even in the office if you have exchanged your chair for a physiotherapy ball. Sit on the ball (5) and tip your pelvis back and forth. You will feel wonderfully relaxed if you do this for five minutes.

BEING BEAUTIFUL – STAYING BEAUTIFUL

"Mirror, mirror on the wall…" Some women have a panic-stricken fear of losing some of their attractiveness with progressing age, while others are very laid-back about this process. How can this be? The more your own self-confidence and self-value are based on an attractive, youthful outward appearance, the harder it generally is to make friends with the aging woman that looks back at you out of the mirror as the years go by. Though the process of aging cannot be stopped, it can be significantly slowed down with the appropriate care. And if you like yourself and are aware of your assets, you will be very relaxed about accepting the first wrinkles as what they actually are: the chronicle of a life lived written in your skin.

Just What is Beauty?

There is a good reason for the saying 'beauty lies in the eye of the beholder'. It is part of human nature that our body, our skin and our hair are subject to the aging process. Just how quickly this happens, how soon signs of age can be seen and how significant these are partly depends on our lifestyle, but also on our inner attitude. For it is entirely up to ourselves whether we feel sorry for ourselves when we look into the mirror and whether every grey hair or every new little wrinkle is registered and is seen as a catastrophe.

These days, hair dyes or make-up can help you look a few years younger in next to no time.

Nowadays there is quite a lot you can do against some signs of aging: hair dyes and cosmetics are subtle aids with which you can easily hide the first harbinger of advancing age. It is quite a simple matter these days to reduce your age by a number of years in visual terms, by using special care products that meet the needs of your skin type, by exercising regularly and by dressing in fashionable, suitable clothes. The elderly matron with a bluish perm, a tweed suit and 'sensible' shoes – for a long time a favourite stereotype among cartoonists – is now becoming an increasingly rare sight.

Nevertheless, the process of aging can't be completely stopped. That's why apart from a healthy diet, good body care, sufficient sleep and some moderate exercise, there is an important aspect that should not be missing from your anti-aging programme: simply learn to like yourself the way you are, so that you can answer the question 'Am I beautiful?' with a definite 'Yes!' 'Mirror, mirror on the wall...' – there are hardly any teenagers who wouldn't want to change something about their physical apperance if it were possible. But many a mature, grown-up woman who is well-balanced, likes and accepts herself as a personality has often accepted her own little quirks as being part of her personality and has learnt to live with them.

It is particularly these women who have a special charisma that they tend to maintain well into a high age. They have found their style, know how they can emphasise their advantages and cleverly hide their weaknesses, and they are at peace with themselves and their looks.

Only if you are aware of your assets are you able to make use of them. If you have always had difficulties with your appearance, try looking at

Women are often their own harshest critics. Why not try it the other way around? Make yourself aware of your best qualities and think about how you could put them to best effect. Your weaknesses, on the other hand, should be treated like disobedient children: lovingly and patiently, without letting them terrorise you…

Just what is beauty?   93

yourself from a different perspective. What would a friend who is kindly disposed towards you compliment you on above all? What would she name as your personal bonus? Your expressive eyes? Your gentle skin? Your long legs? Your infectious laugh? You attractive neck-line or wasplike waist? Your excellent posture? Take some time to look at yourself in the mirror from head to toe and note all your assets.

Don't be too hard on yourself, and don't compare yourself to any ideal images. Forget about the 'must haves' and focus on your 'have gots'. Try to objectively note what is attractive about yourself. Once you've started, you'll be quite surprised at how long this list actually is in the end.

You should get this 'positive list' out every now and then and look at it, for it fulfils two aims: when you are once again moaning about your wobbly thighs or your drooping eyelids, your list will remind you of your assets. You should also consult it every now and then when you are planning your personal care and beauty program or when choosing your clothes. That's how you can check from time to time whether you are still enhancing your assets appropriately, are giving your best physical asset the best care possible and which good points you might be able to emphasise even more.

Yet, there's one thing you shouldn't forget: this is all for your own well-being. You should never let it become a mere obligation. No clever strategist makes use of all available powers at all times. More precisely: whenever you feel like it, you can conceal your tiny waist under a comfortable sweater. There is nothing to be said against doing that – as long as you yourself are aware that you are hiding an enviable good figure beneath it, which you will confidently show off again at the next good opportunity.

HOW YOUR SKIN CHANGES

Our skin is an anatomical wonder: it covers an area of almost thirty square feet, weighs about five pounds and is the largest organ of the human body. As a protecting cover it shields us from the detrimental effects of the environment but at the same time it is a highly sensitive sensory organ. For our skin contains the receptors of our sense of touch that literally make us feeling beings.

It is our skin for example that enables us to register temperature and which at the same time protects us from damage. If it is too hot, our skin perspires – the evaporation cools our body and prevents it from overheating. If it is too cold, we get goose bumps – a relic from former times, when this impulse caused our warming fur to stand on end. At the same time, our blood vessels contract, causing the body to dissipate less heat. Our skin serves to get rid of the metabolism's waste products and it also plays a role in breathing. In addition our skin is a kind of calling card: it clearly reflects how we are feeling at the moment. Short nights are 'rewarded' with dark rings under our eyes, and mental strain is often expressed in the form of impurities. How could we forget that disastrous spot that appeared just before our very first date?

Our skin can cope with all these responsibilities because it consists of three layers: below the outer layer, consisting of tough cells, is the elastic dermis (a thick inner layer) containing sweat glands and sebaceous glands as well as sensory receptors. Below that is the subcutaneous tissue, in which we store water and fat and which simultaneously functions as a padding element. These layers are found on our whole body. However, they are significantly thinner in our face than elsewhere. This is the reason why our face shows clear signs of aging at a particularly early stage.

Our skin ages gradually in a continuous process that begins even before the first wrinkles become visible. Quite a variety of factors are responsible for this: the skin's process of regeneration slows down. With progressing age, our skin gradually loses its ability to store water. And the process of cell renewal is also slowed down. Minor and major misdemeanours that were soon forgotten in younger years leave visible marks as the years progress. To the degree that the collagen content of our skin sinks, its tautness is also reduced. The fat and water levels in the cells change and the fat tissues of the subcutaneous layer become thinner. In addition, the circulation of blood to our skin deteriorates as we age, as a result of which our cells are no longer provided with the substances they need as well as they used to be. All these factors result in our skin needing more intensive care as we age.

From their twenty-fifth year onwards, most women already have the first, subtle lines around their eyes and mouth. These parts of our faces are used most often, so that the elastic tissue begins to slacken the fastest here. By the time your thirtieth birthday is approaching, your skin is already starting to become dryer. The collagen substance in the connective tissue

Collagen is an important constituent of our connective tissue. It ensures our skin is taut. Once the collagen content diminishes, the structure of our skin also changes: its tautness and elasticity are reduced. Elastin, which is chemically related to collagen, has a similar effect. It is an elastic protein that among other things is responsible for keeping our sinews and blood vessels flexible.

begins to harden. Between the age of about thirty and forty, the collagen's ability to swell up and pad the skin is reduced. In addition, the sweat glands and sebaceous glands reduce their productive activity and the renewal of cells in the upper layer of your skin also becomes a much slower process. Your pores become larger, your skin becomes dry more quickly and – especially around your eyes – it becomes thinner. If you wake up with swollen eyes, it now takes much longer for the swelling to subside. And it now also becomes evident whether your veins have a tendency to burst.

After your fortieth birthday, the wrinkles around your eyes and mouth and on your forehead become more pronounced. The reason for this is that your skin is getting dryer and more sensitive. It is losing an increasing amount of elastin, a substance that is important to the structure that supports the skin. Rings under your eyes can now sometimes turn into tear bags. Finally, during and after menopause, your skin undergoes significant changes: fine lines develop into unsightly wrinkles and your skin becomes slacker and uneven. Damage done by the sun years ago now takes its revenge in the form of rough or patchy skin. Various signs of aging set in or become increasingly noticeable.

THE WORST MISDEMEANOURS – FACTORS THAT EXPEDITE THE AGING OF YOUR SKIN

To us, an even, clear and rosy complexion is the epitome of health, beauty and youthful vitality. Our skin above all needs two things so that it can 'radiate' from within: oils and moisture. It consists of billions of cells that are surrounded by a saline fluid. Together, these form a virtually perfect protective system that can, however, only function properly if the top layer of skin is constantly regenerated.

This important process of regeneration takes place at night. New cells are formed and replace the old ones. On their way out, the skin cells gradually become more compact and stable and by the time they reach the outer layer completely consist of horn. These horn cells cover the entire body with a protective layer that helps to hold back sufficient liquid in the skin. In a young person, it takes about a month from the time a new skin cell forms to its arrival at the body's outermost layer. The process becomes slower with progressing age.

Dermatologists differentiate between inner and outer aging of the skin. Inner aging of the skin is a natural process and mostly beyond our influence: the amount of collagen and elastin tissue decreases with the years. In the course of time, our skin gets thinner, dryer and, because the production of pigments decreases, also paler. Simultaneously, the muscles below lose their elasticity.

However, the exact time at which inner aging begins and how fast it progresses depends on a variety of outer factors that are summarised in the term 'outer skin aging'. And we certainly have an influence on these factors! Apart from stress and too little sleep, a bad circulation caused by too little exercise, alcohol consumption, smoking, not drinking enough fluid, pollution, yo-yo diets, too much sun or too many visits to the solarium all number among these factors.

Don't wait until you feel thirsty: thirst is your body's way of showing you that it is lacking fluid. A simple test can help you to find out whether you have to drink more: Pinch the skin on the back of your hand between the thumb and forefinger of your other hand. If a visible fold remains for a few seconds afterwards, your fluid level is too low.

Permanent stress quickly makes you look exhausted. The hormones released in stress situations mobilise the power reserves of your body, and the skin's own collagen forms part of these reserves. As a result, your skin loses its elasticity. We also tend to eat badly and irregularly in stress situations, to smoke, drink more alcohol and coffee and to sleep less – all this is disastrous for our skin.

Not only lack of exercise but also regular consumption of alcohol tends to impair your blood circulation. In addition, alcohol draws fluid and important nutrients out of your skin. This can result in burst blood vessels, deeper wrinkles, and a pale and dull complexion. That's why you should reduce your alcohol consumption and at the same time make sure you drink sufficient liquid over the course of the day (about two to three litres, or four to six pints). Mineral water, unsweetened fruit juices and fruit teas are especially suitable. Water keeps your skin supple and helps the body to get rid of waste products created by metabolism. Apart from getting a lot of exercise in the fresh air, regular visits to the sauna or steam baths are good for your circulation.

If you smoke, you are straining your skin in various ways. It gets thinner and loses its elasticity. Smoking constricts the blood vessels, thus reducing the oxygen supply to the skin. That's why it quickly looks pallid and flaccid. Smokers' skin tends to be affected by impurities and is quick to react with irritation. In addition, a typical pattern of wrinkles develops in the corners of smokers' mouths and around their upper lip that comes from drawing at cigarettes. You would certainly be doing your skin a favour if you gave up smoking. If you are unable or unwilling to do this, you should at least make sure that your diet contains sufficient antioxidants to protect your skin against damage from free radicals.

If you live in a city, you will be familiar with this scenario: you've washed your face in the evening. If you cleanse it afterwards with a cleansing lotion and a cotton wool pad, the pad still turns a brownish grey. Every day, our skin is exposed to considerable strain through pollution. A good day cream, ideally one containing a UV filter, can somewhat alleviate these attacks by harmful substances. Thorough cleansing at the end of each day and a moisturising face mask every now and then are very good for your skin.

Your skin also does not appreciate radical diets: since these tend to be rather unbalanced, your body lacks important nutrients. Your skin also suffers as a result. Because you tend to gain more weight after a crash-diet than you lose through it, your skin is repeatedly stretched significantly and slackens over the course of time. If you then lose weight again, it won't shrink with your weight loss, but will become wrinkly. Instead of trying out dubious miracle diets, it would be better to try to reduce your weight by changing to a sensible diet and exercising regularly.

By far the most skin damage results from exposure to solar radiation. As pleasant as we consider the sun's warming rays on our skin – if you catch too much sun, you will get to feel the damaging power of its rays sooner or later. For your skin never forgets. Every sunburn will cause your skin to age sooner and more distinctly. Every excess of sun causes some damage, and this all adds up as the years go by. Your skin dries out and becomes leathery. In the course of time, more and more pigmentation marks appear and your risk of skin cancer is increased by thoughtless exposure to the sun.

Not only holiday excesses make a significant difference: even daily exposure to the sun on your way to work or shopping strains your skin. Since less melanin (a colorant that naturally protects the skin from the sun) is produced with progressing age, we become more susceptible to the influence of the sun the older we get. A day cream with a UVA filter can be of great value in this regard. More and more dermatologists are now advising against regular solarium tans, because the UVA strain on your skin is also very high there.

If you want to prevent your skin from damage, you should suntan according to the motto: less is more. That means no tanning without protection. And even if you do use protective suntan lotion properly, you should avoid the scalding midday sun, and not stretch the time limit given on the packaging of your lotion. Move into the shade in good time; you will still be exposed to some of the sun's rays.

Allow sufficient time for your skin to gradually get used to the sun. Only then can your body make best use of its inherent protective system: stimulated by the exposure to sun, the outer layer of skin thickens. It forms a so-called light barrier that can filter out and reflect a certain amount of the sun's rays. Your skin is even capable of repairing minor damage immediately. This, however, requires gently becoming accustomed to the sun over a period of at least two weeks; and a precondition is that you don't maltreat your skin with an 'overdose' of sun.

Make sure your suntan lotion and your day cream contain an UVA and UVB filter. While UVB rays burn the skin, UVA rays are a significant cause of premature aging. That's why you should protect yourself against both kinds of rays to the same extent. And don't forget your lips – sun protection is essential for them, too.

The Various Skin Types

The ideal skin care always depends on your individual skin type. That's why your age plays an important role in choosing the appropriate cleansing and care products. Since your skin changes during your life, you can even develop a different skin type depending on your age. That's why it is recommended that you identify your skin type from time to time and – if necessary – adapt your skin care products and cosmetic products accordingly.

Your skin type is primarily determined by the oil content of your skin. The more oil that is produced by the sebaceous glands, the more robust your skin will be. Whereas the skin of children and older people tends to be drier, the sebaceous glands often produce too much oil during puberty, which results in acne.

In general, a distinction is made between four skin types: normal skin, dry skin, oily skin and combination skin. In addition, each of these four types can be more or less sensitive. A simple test will give you the first clues as to which skin type you have: wash your face in the evening and then do not moisturise it. Firmly press a tissue against your face the next morning. If you have oily skin, you will clearly see your facial outlines. If you have combination skin, only your forehead, chin and nose will leave marks on the tissue, not you cheeks. Normal and dry skin will not leave any marks, but dry skin will be red or feel very taut. If you want more evidence, you can additionally try the test described on the following pages.

How the skin types differ in detail and how you can determine them is described in the following paragraphs. If you are still uncertain about your skin type, you can also ask your dermatologist or a licensed beautician.

Healthy, normal skin is well balanced, neither too dry nor too oily. As a rule of thumb, its circulation is very good and it has a sufficient supply of oils and moisture. The pores are mostly rather small, and a tendency for enlarged pores is rare.

Oily skin is the result of the sebaceous glands producing too much oil. The skin is shiny, especially on your chin, nose and forehead, and it feels oily. Oily skin tends to be affected by impurities and infections and even acne. The excessive production of oil frequently leads to blocked pores, which are often enlarged as well. Oily skin often seems pallid, it is thicker, horny and not well supplied with blood. How pronounced oily skin is can vary according to the time of year. A positive side-effect of oily skin is that it generally ages more slowly: because it loses moisture and elasticity less quickly, it is also less subject to wrinkling.

Even though susceptibility to oily skin is a predisposition, the following factors can aggravate the symptoms: stress, pollution, climatic influences, hormone changes, sugary or fatty foods, alcohol consumption, faulty cleansing and care products.

Dry skin can be lacking oils, moisture or even both. It tends to become red, suffer irritations and often reacts very sensitively to environmental influences. Dry skin has very fine pores, a very soft and thin layer of horn that easily flakes. It often feels taut after cleansing. It quickly becomes rough, sometimes it can even split and it often seems pallid. The facial lines become very clear. Dry skin tends to be susceptible to infection, but also tends to produce wrinkles sooner. Especially around your eyes, dry skin quickly loses its elasticity. In general, it tires and slackens much sooner than other skin types. Extreme dryness gives rise to pronounced wrinkles around your mouth and nose and on your neck. That's why dry skin needs very intensive care.

Dry skin reacts extremely sensitively to inappropriate care products, excessive exposure to the sun and marked changes in air temperature or humidity. Because your skin gradually loses its ability to retain water with progressing age, dry skin can become a significant problem in the second half of your life.

By far the most common skin type is the so-called combination skin. Around your cheeks and eyes it tends to be dry and even rough; on the other hand, in the so-called T-zone – forehead, nose and chin – it is oily. There is a gradual transition between the dry and oily parts of the skin which cannot be detected with the naked eye, even though the pores of the oily skin patches frequently tend to be dilated. With this skin type, blackheads, impurities and infections occur mostly in the T-zone.

All skin types, even oily skin, can dry out under unfavourable conditions such as inappropriate skin care or too much sun. With progressing age, your skin becomes more prone to dryness. A lot of people with dry skin often assume that their skin is also sensitive because of this.

WHICH SKIN TYPE DO I HAVE?

For each of the following questions, tick the answer that applies the most closely to your skin. At the end, add up how often you ticked A, B, C, or D. The letter you ticked most often corresponds to your skin type.

How does your face feel when you wash it with soap and water?

A Normal.

B Pleasantly refreshed.

C It is taut and itches.

D Partly pleasant and partly dry.

Is your skin affected by spots and impurities?

A Occasionally.

B Yes, frequently.

C Very rarely.

D Forehead, skin and nose are frequently affected, other areas hardly ever.

How does your skin react to toners?

A No problems.

B It feels very refreshed.

C With an unpleasant stinging.

D A bit of both: parts feel very refreshed, others sting.

What does your skin look like when you look in the mirror in the afternoon?

A Just as fresh as in the morning.

B It is shiny.

C It is flaky in a few places.

D My forehead and nose are shiny.

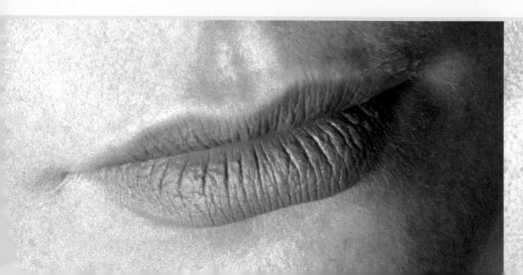
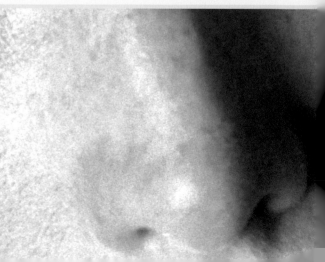

What does your skin feel like when you apply a rich lotion over night?

A Good.

B It is very shiny and seems oily.

C Very pleasant, supple and relaxed.

D Cheeks and eyes feel very pleasant; forehead, nose and chin are very shiny.

EVALUATION:

Mostly A: You have healthy, normal skin.

Mostly B: Your skin is likely to be oily.

Mostly C: You tend to have dry skin.

Mostly D: Your complexion is the classical 'combination' skin type.

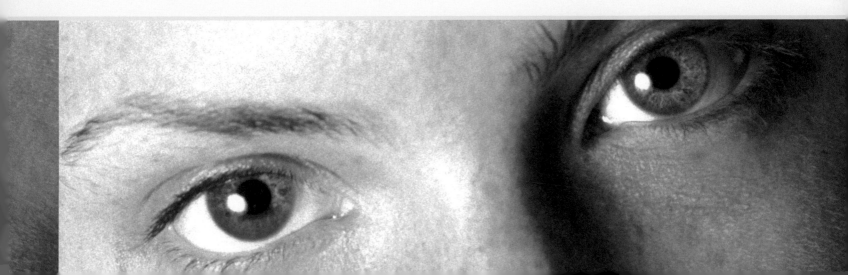

However, the sensitivity of your skin is not connected to a specific skin type, but occurs in people with all types of skin. Sensitive skin reacts very quickly and very strongly to environmental influences such as the sun, very low temperatures and wind: irritation and redness are sure signs of this. In addition, allergic reactions to perfumes or preservatives in cosmetic products, for example, occur to an increasing extent. Sensitive skin is often characterised by a very thin, fragile and fine structure and tends to have dilated blood vessels.

Sensitive skin normally remains sensitive throughout your whole life. But even more robust types of skin also go through hard times occasionally: if your skin is affected by illness, psychological strain, too much sun or stress, it will become tired more quickly, look pallid, pale and badly supplied with blood and will be quick to react to environmental influences with irritation. Skin strained in such ways normally only needs some relaxation and will quickly recuperate with appropriate care and attention.

WHICH SKIN CARE FOR WHICH SKIN TYPE?

If you have normal skin, you can count yourself lucky. Your skin care is comparatively simple and uncomplicated. However, with progressing age you should pay more attention to it because it will become drier and lose elasticity. Environmental strains can also upset your basically easy-to-handle skin. With appropriate care products, it should be a simple matter for you to feel good and carefree about your own skin for a long time.

Even uncomplicated skin regularly needs gentle cleansing to remove dirt and traces of make-up. Rinse your face with tepid water and then treat it with a gentle cleansing lotion. Refresh your skin afterwards with a skin toner. Avoid the delicate area around your eyes. The culmination of your daily care program should be a good moisturising cream that you gently massage into your face with your fingertips.

Oily skin is more robust than other skin types and does not age as quickly. Yet, it is no less demanding in terms of skin care. Oily skin mostly has large pores and tends to be affected by blackheads and impurities. That's why thorough cleansing is the be-all and end-all of skin care. Unfortunately, oily skin tends to be affected by spots and impurities. Be sure to keep your

Our skin consists of three layers: the epidermis, the dermis and the subcutaneous tissue. These layers not only effectively protect us against damaging environmental influences, but also accurately mirror our state of well-being.

hands away from the inflamed areas, however difficult this may be. Dab some disinfecting, anti-inflammatory cream on them, but don't squeeze them! This could leave nasty scars.

Yet even for oily skin, the care products shouldn't be too aggressive: the best products for this type of skin are those that gently remove oil from the surface and that open the pores without drying out the skin. For even oily skin can suffer from a lack of moisture and can possibly even react to this by producing even more oil to balance out the deficiency.

Gently cleansing gels and lotions remove excess oils and impurities and at the same time gently disinfect your skin. Creams containing marigold have an anti-inflammatory effect. Regular exfoliation helps to open up the blocked pores, and can thus be good for oily skin. Oil-free moisturising products are recommended to protect the skin from drying out.

If your skin is susceptible to inflammation, you should avoid touching your face with your hands so as not to additionally irritate your skin. You should make sure that your diet is balanced and not too fatty and that you drink a lot of fluid. Exercise can also be good for your skin – but do so without wearing make-up, so that your skin can breathe.

Dry skin is a case for concern because it is very thin and cannot retain a great deal of moisture. Yet generally, dry skin also has a very low oil content. Daily showers and excessively long baths can virtually dry out your skin. If you can't do without them, you should at least pamper your skin with some additional care afterwards. Soap and washing lotions also strain your skin. That's why it is very important to moisturise your skin afterwards with creams or oils.

Oily products aren't very popular because they often leave a shiny trace behind them and are only absorbed slowly. However, a pure moisturiser isn't suitable for dry and oil-less skin, because it makes the skin swell up, thus extracting more moisture from the lower layers. Make sure you use a skin care range that is specifically tailored to the needs of dry skin. A good nourishing cream that should contain more oil than water is especially important, because it enables your skin to retain more moisture in the upper layers.

Avoid care products containing alcohol or detergent, as well as strong face tonics and all cleansing products that have a strong oil-extracting

Even if you are blessed with normal skin: never go to bed with make-up on. Especially eye make-up should be gently but thoroughly removed before you go to bed, otherwise you will risk waking up with irritated and swollen skin.

effect. Rather, use a gentle cleansing gel or a cleansing lotion with a high cream or oil content. Either remove the care product with a cotton wool pad or rinse it off with cold water: this will additionally stimulate the circulation of blood. Your eye make-up remover should contain oil, but shouldn't be too greasy so as not to irritate the area around the eyes. If you want to do your skin a favour, pamper it regularly with a moisturising mask.

If you have dry skin, it is especially important to provide it with complex sun protection early on. In addition, you should drink a lot of fluid and make sure that you take in sufficient essential fatty acids with your diet. Regular exercise in the fresh air is good for your skin, but you should avoid extreme climatic conditions such as intense heat or icy cold weather if possible.

If you have a classic combination skin, you don't necessarily need different care products for the two skin patches. When you use a moisturising cream, you should mainly apply this to the dry patches on your cheeks and only thinly rub it into the T-zone. Occasional exfoliation is good for the impure skin of the T-zone. However, when using exfoliation and cleansing products you should generally avoid your drier cheeks and the area around your eyes, so as not to dry these out even more. It is very important that you do not go to bed wearing make-up. If you then also ensure that your skin is sufficiently protected against the sun's rays in good time, have a balanced, fat-free diet and drink enough, then you shouldn't really have many problems with your combination skin.

When you are thinking about the daily care for your very sensitive skin, you need to keep in mind that your skin's natural balance can be upset by seemingly insignificant factors. Sensitive skin can quickly become very taut and is often red. In order to protect and support the skin's self-defences, it is necessary to use very gentle care products. Study the list of ingredients carefully: the products should contain a lot of oils and moisture in order to supply the skin sufficiently and to protect it against irritation from the outside.

You should observe the following as a rule of thumb: the fewer the ingredients, the better. Preservatives contained in cosmetics and care products serve the purpose of making these preparations last longer. Invading germs shouldn't be given the opportunity to multiply. Yet, if you have very sensitive skin, you had best avoid products with such aggressive ingredients. You should also avoid heavily scented creams and lotions: the perfume oils can irritate your skin unnecessarily. The same applies to essential oils. You should test substances containing fruit acids on an inconspicuous part of your skin, since they can strongly irritate it.

Because your skin on the whole become drier as you age, you should keep a more careful eye on whether your skin reddens or begins to flake once you are beyond the age of forty. These are the first tell-tale signals that your skin is becoming increasingly drier. In this case, you should seek advice from a beautician to find out whether the care products you have been using still meet the needs of your skin or whether you should adapt them to the changing demands of your skin.

If you notice the first signs of dry skin, start using only gently cleansing products and, ideally, completely go without soap. Now at the latest is also the time to get rid of any facial toner based on alcohol. When exfoliating your skin, you need to be especially careful: exfoliating products shouldn't be used too frequently and shouldn't be too aggressive. You should also be careful about using very hot or very cold water, in order to avoid burst blood vessels. A reliable suntan lotion is indispensable. Ideally, you will start using a day cream with a sun protection factor (SPF).

More mature skin needs additional care. With each cleansing – no matter how gentle – dead skin flakes, oils and make-up remains are removed. The skin always also loses some moisture in the process. Whereas this loss can easily be balanced out when you are young, mature skin is grateful for external help. So it is important to carefully moisturise your entire body after having a shower or a bath. You should treat your skin to a good moisturiser that you apply generously to your face, neck and neckline in the mornings and in the evenings. If you want to pamper your skin from time to time with a mask, use moisturising products that do not dry.

Some care products containing liposomes are specifically designed to meet the demands of more mature skin. Here, we are dealing with the tiniest of hollow spheres with an outer shell of oil that are filled with a combination of water and nutrients. These microscopically minute containers can penetrate into much deeper layers of your skin and are supposed to deliver the substances to where they are really needed. At the same time, their oil coating is supposed to somewhat pad out the upper layer of skin.

HOME-MADE COSMETICS

If you like using home-made cosmetics, you can also perhaps try the following recipes. Please note that freshly prepared cosmetic products without preservatives don't keep very long and must be stored in a cool, dark place. Wherever possible, try to use products from controlled organic farming or from the chemists or drug store.

Even home-made cosmetic products can sometimes cause undesirable skin reactions. That's why you should test their tolerance by applying the finished product to the inside of your elbow in the evening and leave it on overnight. You should really only use a home-made product if your skin shows no irritation the next morning.

For Oily Skin

Exfoliating Scrub with Almond Meal

Directions: Use once a week. Mix 150 ml (5 oz) of milk, a cup of almond meal and 20 ml ($^2/_3$ oz) of almond oil to a smooth paste. Apply this mixture to the face and gently massage in with circular movements. Then rinse off with tepid water.

Facial Toner with Sage

Pour boiling water over four tablespoons of sage leaves and let brew for 10 minutes. Pour the mixture through a sieve and let it cool off. Pour the liquid into a bottle, add 40 ml ($1^1/_3$ oz) of alcohol (70%) and four drops of sage oil. Then shake the mixture thoroughly.

Cleansing Milk with Yoghurt

Mix 250 g ($8^1/_2$ oz) of yoghurt with 20 ml ($^2/_3$ oz) each of sage tea and balm tea. Let the mixture rest in the refrigerator for 72 hours and then add two drops of clove essence.

For Dry Skin

Cleansing Cucumber Lotion

Grate half a peeled cucumber and strain it through a sieve. Then blend with the juice of half a lemon, 60 ml (2 oz) of carrot juice and 40 ml ($1^1/_3$ oz) of almond oil for a wonderfully moisturising effect.

Moisturising Cream with Banana

Mash half a ripe banana with a fork and mix with 2 teaspoonfuls of neutral cream. Then blend the mixture with one tablespoon each of olive oil and lemon juice until it is smooth.

Muesli Mask

Boil six tablespoons of finely chopped pumpkin in 300 ml ($10^1/_2$ oz) of sweet cream at low heat. When the fruit becomes soft, add four tea-spoons of oat flakes, allow the mixture to cool off and apply to your face while still warm. Leave on for 30 minutes at the longest, then rinse off thoroughly.

Yeast Bath for Smooth Skin

Rough and dry skin can be pampered smooth by a bath: dissolve 125 g ($4^1/_4$ oz) of fresh yeast in about $1^1/_2$ litres (3 pints) of warm water and add this mixture to your bath. Don't bathe too hot or too long.

For Mature Skin

Avocado-whey Cleansing Milk

Mix 100 g ($3^1/_2$ oz) of oatmeal with 400 ml (14 oz) of whey to make a smooth paste. Then add 35 ml ($1^1/_4$ oz) of avocado oil and 30 mg (1 oz) of almond meal and mix thoroughly. Fill into clean glass bottles and store in a cool place.

Potato Mask

Mash two boiled potatoes, add three teaspoons of milk and an egg yolk to make a paste. Heat this mixture in a double boiler and apply it to your skin while still warm. Leave for about 15 minutes, then rinse it off your face with tepid water.

Regenerating Mask with Curd Cheese

Mix four tablespoons of curd cheese together with a large egg yolk, two teaspoons of glucose and the juice of a small orange. Beat the egg white until it is firm, and gently mix with the paste. Leave out the area around the eyes and mouth when applying this mixture. Leave for about half an hour, then rinse off with tepid water and rinse your face again with cold water afterwards.

For Sensitive Skin

Cleansing Oil with Parsley

Put two tablespoons of freshly chopped parsley into a clean bottle together with 100 ml ($3^1/_2$ oz) of high-quality olive oil, and leave to draw for about a week. Sieve the mixture and heat the oil together with 100 g ($3^1/_2$ oz) of lanolin and 60 ml (2 oz) of almond oil. Stir until smooth. Then fill into a glass bottle.

Cream with Avocado

Beat two egg whites until firm. Mix the two egg yolks with 60 ml (2 oz) of avocado oil, a pinch of salt, some cider vinegar and a little lemon juice. Afterwards mix the beaten egg white under the cream and fill into clean little cream tubs.

Quick Cucumber Mask

Mash half a washed cucumber with its skin and mix it with four level table-spoons of curd cheese. Apply to your face and neck, leave for about twenty minutes and rinse off with cold water.

Calming Camomile Compress

Pour half a litre (a pint) of boiling water over two to three tablespoons of camomile leaves. Allow to brew for about ten minutes, pour through a sieve and let it cool off. When the liquid is lukewarm, soak a cloth in it and cover your face with it. Leave it on your face for about 10 to 15 minutes, then apply a cold compress for about three minutes.

Miracle Creams: What Can They Really Do?

Whether you are flipping through a magazine or going into a perfumery – hardly a week goes by in which a new 'miracle weapon' against wrinkles isn't advertised. Creams and lotions, ampoules and capsules are supposed to wipe out the signs of our age and give our skin its youthful looks back. Year after year, the cosmetics industry makes profits that run into billions by exploiting women's fear of aging.

And the messages do in fact sound quite convincing: new, high-tech formulas, developed in modern laboratories, based on scientific research, dermatologically tested – catchwords such as these can be found over and over again. Another very popular statement is that some product or other has been successfully proven to 'reduce wrinkles by up to 50 percent'. Who wouldn't like that? All these statements might even be true – yet they cannot guarantee the desired effects.

Frequently, the units of measurement on which these tests are based are so small that the results – which often seem ever so impressive when expressed in terms of figures – can rarely be detected with the naked eye. And sometimes, when new cosmetic products are being tested, the subjects are not allowed to use any cosmetic products for several weeks before the tests begin.

Can you imagine what your skin would feel like after fourteen days without any toner or moisturiser? It is therefore hardly surprising that the subjects – after such a 'dry patch' – have the impression that their skin feels 'significantly smoother' or 'noticeably more supple' after using the new product. After such a time, even salad oil would be quite likely to have similarly noticeable effects.

On the other hand, however, some effects of the new products are also kept quiet – and for good reason: the testing regulations for cosmetic products are far less strict than those for medication. So rather than putting a new product through a lengthy licensing procedure, thereby significantly delaying its entry on the market, a cosmetics company will probably do anything to avoid its new product from being too closely associated with highly potent medication. Thus, we can't completely rule out that some anti-aging products have much more far-reaching effects than those indicated on their packaging.

Therefore, it is sensible to have a certain amount of scepticism and caution when using such anti-aging products, which are also often extremely expensive. Before spending horrendous amounts on such a product, you should ask for a sample or – if packaged samples aren't available – for some of the product to be filled into a little pot so that you can test it at home. Even if a good friend is full of praise for a new miracle product, ask her for a small sample of it first. For you should always test (on a not readily visible part of your body) whether a cream has practically no effect, or maybe even far too strong an effect, before applying it to your face. The skin on the inside of your elbow, behind your ear or along your hairline is very suitable for such a test because it tends to be just as sensitive as your face. Apply some of the product there in the evening before going to bed. If your skin reacts with redness, itching, or tautness, there's only one thing you can do: avoid that cream!

You should be cautious with any product that removes the top layer of skin in order to expose the layer of skin below with its more youthful appearance. Firstly, your skin often reacts with irritation to such deep exfoliation and secondly, it can't be completely ruled out that your skin, which is thereby robbed of its protective outer layer, will become extremely sensitive to the sun.

Even if it is ever so convenient, try to avoid taking cream out of a pot with your bare fingers. You might infect the product with germs or bacteria. Even if your friend would like to test your day cream, don't let her use her fingers in your pot of cream. You should rather use a spatula or a small spoon to fill a sample into a clean pot.

How to Make Beautiful Eyes Shine

'Here's lookin' at you, kid...' Over the decades, there are sure to have been millions of female viewers that secretly look for a tissue when tough Rick (alias Humphrey Bogart) whispers these words to the love of his life Elsa (Ingrid Bergman) in the film classic *Casablanca*.

There are a few tricks you can use to make tired patches around your eyes disappear quickly. Bags under your eyes can be treated with an eye mask made from cooled curd cheese or raw, grated potatoes – leave this on for twenty minutes and then rinse it off with tepid water. Swollen eyelids disappear if you put tea compresses on them: pour boiling water over a camomile or breakfast tea teabag, then place it in the freezer to cool it down. Dab your eyes and the surrounding area with the teabag afterwards.

It is not without reason that our eyes are described as the windows of the soul. They are our most expressive means of non-verbal communication. Beautiful eyes can be real 'eye-catchers', the attractive centre of a face. For this reason they deserve special attention and care. Around our eyes, the skin is particularly thin and therefore very prone to little wrinkles and swellings. The small blood vessels are just below the surface, and the layer of collagen and elastin tissue is much thinner there than in other parts of our body. Also, the skin around the eyes contains fewer sebaceous glands, which is why this area dries out much faster.

Major and minor 'beauty transgressions' show up the most clearly around our eyes. Several other factors also leave their marks in the sensitive area around our eyes: working at the computer, smoky rooms, make-up, or setting out on an extended car journey without wearing sunglasses – all these strain the eyes and the area around them.

That's why you should protect your eyes against the sun and use a special eye cream in your daily care programme. Conventional creams and facial masks are often not suitable for this sensitive area. They often contain perfumes or emulsifiers that irritate the skin around your eyes; redness or stinging can be the result. In general, creams described as 'hypoallergenic' are very tolerable – they are mixed carefully and are specifically adapted to the sensitive skin around your eyes. For additional protection, you should wear good sunglasses (prescription glasses if necessary) with a broad frame to protect the area of your face beside your eyes.

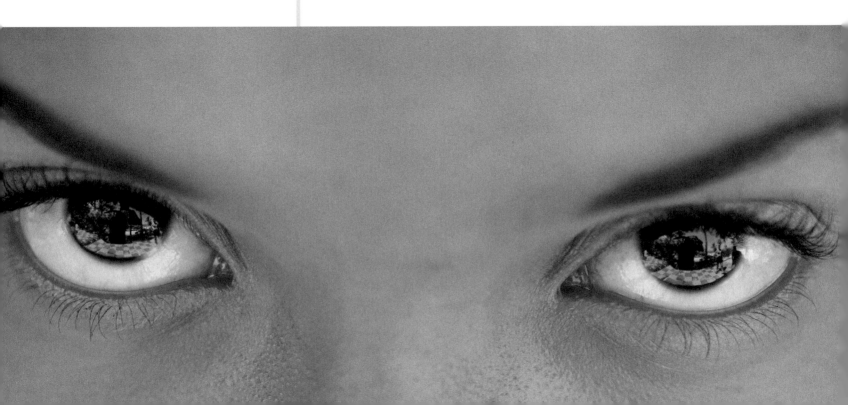

If the area around your eyes isn't extremely sensitive, you can use a light moisturising cream containing an SPF on your face and around your eyes during the day. After thorough cleansing in the evening (make-up remains strain the eyes and can lead to impurities) you should pamper your eyes with a rich eye cream overnight. By the way, your eyelids also need some extra care, since they work very hard every day: by blinking about twenty times per minute they moisturise your eyes, remove minute dirt particles and thus ensure clear vision.

To avoid unnecessarily straining this delicate area around your eyes, you should treat it very carefully:

- Always generously leave out this area when using facial masks.

- Don't massage creams and gels into this area; dab them on and perhaps pat them in gently.

- Be careful not to stretch or pull the thin skin around your eyes when you are massaging your face.

- Remove make-up gently: put make-up remover onto a soft cotton wool pad and gently stroke from the eyebrows towards the eyelashes. Then use a fresh pad with make-up remover and move from the outer to the inner corner of your eye without pressure until all make-up has been removed.

If your eyes are very sensitive, you should also avoid applying even special eye creams directly below the eye or on the lid. Rather, spread small amounts of the products around the edge of your eye socket. Through blinking and natural eye movements, the cream will be transported towards the eye but won't get into it as easily.

- If you've made a small mistake while applying make-up, don't just remove it completely and start from scratch. Often a wet cotton bud can be used to make the necessary corrections.

- Do you tend to get bags around your eyes? Then you should always keep a teaspoon in your freezer. Gently stroke over these blemishes until they disappear. Gel teething rings for babies also make excellent eye compresses when cooled.

Do You Have Problems with Your Eyes?

With progressing age, you will often be confronted with problems with your eyes that are not only of a cosmetic nature. Our eyesight can weaken – especially when it comes to short distances – because the lenses of our eyes start losing elasticity just as the rest of our body does. It becomes increasingly difficult to focus on objects that are within a short distance of our eyes. Mostly, this age-related far-sightedness is first noticed when reading. Since a number of pretty and fashionable reading spectacles have become available which fit into any handbag, even with their case, or can be worn around the neck on a decorative chain if they are to be used more frequently, age-related far-sightedness no longer poses any real problem.

If you have had dark rings under your eyes for a long period of time, you should consult a doctor. This type of discolouring can be caused by a liver or kidney deficiency.

Other age-related eye complaints such as cataract or glaucoma, however, can lead to serious impairment and even to blindness. Research has shown that susceptibility for these illnesses can be reduced by means of a healthy, balanced diet. Especially a good supply of antioxidants or 'radical catchers' such as vitamin A, C, and E as well as betacarotene are of vital importance. Have your eyes examined regularly by an ophthalmologist so that serious disorders can be detected and treated at an early stage.

Susceptibility to dry eyes, which a lot of women notice after menopause, is not really dangerous, but nevertheless rather annoying. Even if you have never yet had any problems with your contact lenses, you might have difficulties now, and even eyes that were quite healthy suddenly begin

Medical eye drops should not be used for an extended period of time, unless your doctor has explicitly told you to do so. Just like nose drops, your body can become accustomed to them and this will aggravate the symptoms in the long term.

to burn, itch or redden. The reason for this often lies in the reduced tear production. Sometimes it can help to increase the humidity around your house, e.g. by using a humidifier. You should also protect your eyes against draughts, take frequent breaks while working at the computer and blink consciously and frequently, as well as wearing sunglasses outside, even when the sky is cloudy. If none of this helps, you should consult a doctor. You can get little phials containing artificial tears that you can put into your eyes. But before using these or eye drops, you should seek medical advice.

GLASSES AND CONTACT LENSES

'I need glasses!' For a lot of women, this realisation is something of a shock. Yet once you have become accustomed to the idea, you will see that there is no need to panic. Wearing glasses is no longer immediately associated with the notion of having four eyes or resembling an owl. These days, there is such a wide variety of attractive, fashionable (and even affordable) frames available that a lot of women have discovered glasses as an accessory. Take your time trying out different shapes and models. Take your husband or a good friend along and look at the selection at your leisure. Get some free advice on which frames might suit the con-

EXERCISING YOUR EYES

There are various exercising methods that alternately train and relax your eye muscles; these are supposed to help against defective vision and tired eyes. The best known of these is the Bates method.

In this method, your eyes are alternately stimulated and relaxed – by regular blinking, focussing exercises, sudden changes from near objects to distant ones and back again, and by relaxation exercises. If you are interested in learning this method, you should try to acquire it with professional instruction.

The following simple relaxation exercise for your eyes is based on the Bates method (but make sure to remove your glasses or contact lenses first!). Rub your hands together for half a minute until they are warm. Place the palms of your hands over your eyes, but without touching them. Concentrate on your breathing and focus on the darkness behind your eyelids, without opening your eyes.

tours of your face. In this way, you will gradually narrow down the choice to a handful of favourites and can then make a firm final decision.

You should first decide on the following:

- Do you want rimless glasses or a frame?

- If a frame: Should it be metal or plastic?

- Which shape matches your face and your hairstyle?

- If you are thinking of a coloured frame: which colour harmonises with your complexion, your make-up and your wardrobe?

Make sure that the glasses you chose don't emphasise drooping or slack features of your face. Cat's eye or butterfly shapes give a longer look to your face. The top edge of the frame should be level with your eyebrows. And if you are not able to decide between two models, that is no great problem: a lot of women swear by their 'spare' pair of spectacles.

However, if you can't warm to the thought of wearing glasses at all, you should seek advice from a good optician about the various kinds of contact lenses available. The variety stretches from individually adapted long-life lenses to standardised disposable one-day lenses that you simply throw away after use in the evening. A distinction is also made between hard and soft contact lenses.

Which type of lens is best suited to your needs can only be determined in an in-depth consultation. You will often be subjected to a test at first to determine if you have enough tear fluid. Most opticians will allow you to test various lens models (mostly disposable ones) for a few hours so that you can find out if you can in fact grow accustomed to them.

You should practise inserting and removing the lenses yourself under professional instruction, especially if you are far-sighted since you have difficulties seeing things the closer they get to your eyes. Sensitive eyes often react to contact lenses with irritation and redness. Even if you decide in favour of contact lenses, you will additionally need a pair of glasses for emergencies, such as a lost lens or extended sessions in smoky rooms. You should also wear your glasses on long journeys by air, since the dry air in the cabin can make contact lenses painful to wear.

BEAUTIFUL LIPS

You should pay special attention to your lips, in order to protect them from premature aging and other damage. Because the skin on your lips has no sweat glands or sebaceous glands and is much thinner than on most other parts of our body, it loses moisture especially quickly. This often results in chapped lips and small wrinkles. These unwelcome harbingers of aging become deeper and more pronounced if you don't consistently take action. For this reason, your mouth should have its place in your daily care program.

It is especially important to protect your lips against drying out. The sun, wind and cold put the delicate skin on your lips under a lot of strain – that's why they should be well protected when you venture outside. A lip balm that seals the natural oils in your lips can be very useful in this regard. Make sure that it is a long-lasting type so that you don't have to constantly apply it. And make sure that your lip balm also contains sun protection and a UV filter, for the delicate skin on your lips contains only small quantities of the sun protection colorant melanin and is thus highly susceptible to damage from the sun.

If you use lipstick regularly, your skin already has a certain sun protection. As a general rule, the less transparent your lipstick is and the more colour pigments it contains, the better its protection. According to an American research project, women who apply a covering lipstick several times a day have a significantly lower risk of acquiring cancer of the lips.

You should avoid anything that strains the delicate skin of your lips and around them: exfoliating products and other products that irritate the skin should not be applied on or around the mouth. Lose flakes of skin can be

You shouldn't simply moisturise dry lips by licking them. As a result of the constant change between moisture and dryness, even more moisture is extracted from the lips – a vicious circle. It is better to use a long-lasting lip balm or a good lipstick and apply it regularly. You should always carry your lipstick with you.

best removed from the lips by gently massaging them without pressure using a soft, wet toothbrush. If you tend to chew on your lower lip when solving tricky problems, you should try to stop doing this. By the way: if you draw strongly on cigarettes, you will get deep wrinkles around your mouth and your upper lip in the long term.

CARING FOR YOUR NECK AND CLEAVAGE

The neck and hands generally have the reputation of being the most telltale signs of a woman's true age – which is a good reason to include the delicate, thin skin of your neck and cleavage into your daily care programme at an early stage. The skin around your neck loses a great deal of its elasticity with advancing years, because its reserves of collagen and elastin tissues is gradually depleted. And because the skin only contains hardly any fat cells, it also becomes dry and rough very easily. Your cleavage also needs thorough care and special attention. The skin in this area is also very delicate and sensitive. That's why wrinkles in this area are clearly visible.

Treat your neck and your cleavage as well as you treat your face, and avoid anything that might stretch or pull the sensitive tissue in this area. In your daily care programme, you should apply the product you use from the bottom upwards. When you massage in a rich cream afterwards, you should also begin with your cleavage and then gradually move up to your neck. The moisturiser you use for your neck and cleavage should also contain an SPF and a UV filter to prevent skin damage.

You should be reluctant to use exfoliating products in this area, since the skin is very thin. For additional care, you could occasionally apply special neck creams or pamper the delicate skin with a rich facial oil. Regular exercise, for example yoga, can also be very helpful. Alternate hot and cold compresses are also good for your neck. For a taut cleavage, use the shower nozzle to spray cold water onto your chest in circular movements just before getting out of the shower.

To avoid folds and wrinkles, you should also pay attention to your posture. Don't let your chin fall onto your chest, and don't pull your head back between your shoulders. By the way: for your neck, the best position for sleeping is on your back. Purchase a U-shaped pillow and see if you can sleep in this position.

You should be aware of radical weight loss: particularly slim women often show signs of aging sooner. A bit of padding on the bones, on the other hand, pads your skin, fills out little wrinkles and help conceal the fact that your skin is undergoing a process of transformation.

If you are not at all satisfied with your neck, there are a few cunning tricks you can use to hide it or simply divert attention away from it. Purchase a few scarves and shawls. Soft, flowing materials such as silk, chiffon or delicate velvet are the most flattering. Here are a few hints to help you hide your neck:

- Maintain your posture! Stand up straight, without straightening the small of your back. Imagine you were a puppet: on top of your head there is the loop through which a thread runs. This imaginary thread doesn't force you into a rigid position. But in this position, your head is automatically straight and your neck extended. Your neck will not only look less wrinkly, but your whole body will have a more youthful and energetic appearance than if you were to walk around with your eyes and chin lowered.

- Cunning distractions are the key to success. Why not dare to wear some lavish ornaments for a change? Long chains slung round your neck several times, rows of pearls or opulent necklaces attract looks and distract attention from your neck. Conspicuous brooches or ear-rings have the same effect. On the other hand, you should only make use of one highlight at a time, otherwise the profusion of eye-catchers will neutralise the desired effect.

- Astutely chosen collars can also effectively hide your neck. Sweaters with a high collar or polo neck cover slackened patches of skin and can look very feminine if you combine them with a chain, brooch or scarf. Jackets or blouses with high collars, e.g. Indian or Nehru style, are also very becoming.

- Take a long, soft silk scarf, fold it over and wrap it round your neck. Pull the loose ends through the loop. Draped into the V-cut of a pullover or into a blouse, the scarf will hide your neck in a flattering manner.

- A more conservative look is generated if you knot the scarf ends once and then pull apart the material above the knot.

- If you have a more sportive outfit, the good old bandanna will work very well: fold it diagonally and then fold it into a strip 2 to 3 inches wide, beginning from the tip. Warp it round your neck and tie it in a knot at the back. Bandannas look good with shirts, too.

- Fold a square scarf diagonally, put it round your neck with the tip on your chest, wrap the two ends around your neck and knot them in front under the tip of the scarf. This will help you to nicely fill blouse or shirt collars. A classic is to wear a pearl necklace over the scarf.

- A long scarf wrapped around your neck several times can also be very flattering. For special occasions, you can create an unusual ornament with a soft silk scarf and a ring or bangle: put the scarf

Essential Oil Massages for Your Face and Neck

Gentle massages stimulate tired areas of skin as well as their blood flow and metabolism, and have a relaxing effect. A gentle massage with essential oils, is therefore not only good for your face, neck and cleavage, but also for your mood.

Products such as patchouli, incense, lavender, sandalwood and geranium oils are all supposed to prevent premature aging of the skin. It is very important, however, that you **never** apply pure essential oils (as you might use them for your aroma lamps) to your skin, but only use products that are specifically designed for massaging purposes. You can get these for example in health shops, at some chemists and pharmacies or in shops selling natural cosmetics. There you will also be advised if you want to make your own mixtures.

Most oils would irritate your skin far too much if applied undiluted. That's why they must be diluted with a carrier oil before you apply them. Jojoba oil, for example (good with dry and sensitive skin), or wheat germ oil (good with dry, mature and strained skin as well as with scars) are highly suitable. If you want to mix your own oil, you should add three drops of essential oil to 15 ml ($^1/_2$ oz) of carrier oil and mix well. If you tolerate this mixture well, you can gradually increase the essential oil to a maximum of nine drops. The mixture should be stored in glass bottles in a cool place protected from direct sunlight.

For the massage you should tie your hair back and take off your top. Cleanse your skin thoroughly before beginning the massage. Put a few drops of the oil into your hands to warm it, and then spread it with long, sweeping regular strokes from your cleavage, over your shoulders, up your neck, across your chin and cheeks to your forehead. Massage until the oil is completely spread and your skin is pleasantly warm.

You should massage your face and neck particularly gently so as not to stretch your sensitive skin. Make sure to avoid contact with your eyes during the massage.

around your neck and pull the two ends through the ring. Then take the ends and wrap them around the ring and through the middle again. Depending on where you position the ring, the scarf will either be more open with short ends, or is closer-fitting with long ends. With the second variation, you can also place the ring on your shoulder and drape one end of your scarf down your back and one down your front. If the material is very smooth, you might want to fix it to your outfit with a small safety pin so that you don't lose the ring.

Looking Younger with the Right Make-up

Especially women who spend a lot of time in the sun before their thirtieth birthday tend to be affected by hyperpigmentation as they progress in age. This is a kind of discolouring in some places caused by an excess of melanin. Sun marks, age marks and moles are often annoying. Rather than attempting to 'remove' them with chemical bleaches or a bleach based on natural products, you should consult your dermatologist or experiment with foundation to see whether you can't hide the unsightly marks in this way.

Obviously make-up can't really make you any younger. But it can make you look younger and more relaxed in next to no time, which in turn will make you feel better.

You should also attempt to keep up with time when it comes to your make-up. Some women stick to the make-up procedure of their youth for their entire life. But what might look good on a twenty-year-old doesn't necessarily look good on a forty-year-old. In addition, our complexion changes with the years and the first grey hairs also have a strong influence on our looks. That's why you should critically scrutinise your make-up habits and adapt your make-up to the circumstances.

Sometimes, it is quite sufficient to change a hue in colour or to use a different lipstick. As a rule of thumb: soft, muted colours look more natural on older skin than bright colours do. You should be particularly careful with fashionable 'bombshells'. This applies to eye shadows just as much as to lipsticks. If in doubt, you had best leave the metallic blue, bright pink or intensively radiant greens to teenagers – a touch of gold, bronze, plum or apricot tend to look much more flattering on more mature skin.

With advancing age, our skin tends to become irregular and patchy. Properly applied, a suitable foundation and powder can give you an immaculate, even complexion. If you then manage to deliberately highlight the right places and cleverly emphasise your assets, you will seem naturally younger and more beautiful. In general, subtle make-up looks younger than a face completely pasted over that easily takes on a mask-like look. A few basic hints at the beginning:

● Try not to apply make-up under pressure, but take your time. You will be rewarded for your care: perfectly applied make-up will last the whole day and can easily be freshened up. It also only takes a few moments for it to be transformed into an elegant evening make-up: carefully rework your mouth and add a highlight to the middle of your lips with some gloss. Then apply some slightly shimmering powder to your neck, shoulders and cleavage. If you feel like it, you could also slightly (!) intensify your blusher and put on some perfume.

- The ideal place for doing your make-up is where there is daylight, so that you can critically examine your attempts under realistic circumstances. If that isn't possible, the next best alternative is harsh artificial light: if you look good in that, more flattering light conditions will be even more to your advantage ...

- You should always wash your hands thoroughly before applying make-up to avoid irritation through dirt or germs.

- Especially in the case of more mature skin, less is often in fact more. So generally speaking, you will not be doing yourself a favour at all if you try to 'cover up' wrinkles with foundation and powder: in the course of the day or the evening, these products will settle in the wrinkles and emphasise their contours.

- After using a moisturiser, it is best to wait for about fifteen minutes before continuing with your make-up. Then the other products won't be absorbed by your skin as quickly.

FOUNDATION

Perfect make-up is not possible without the right foundation. Quite in contrast to popular belief, this does not have to be applied to cover your whole face – this could easily look mask-like and unnatural. If you want to apply foundation to a large area of your skin, you should always work from the centre to the outside and then only gently pat it in below the eyes. Your skin should be visible through the foundation, so that your face doesn't look 'painted'.

Perfect foundation is invisible. That's why you shouldn't test a foundation on the back of your hand (since the skin there is often darker than your general complexion), but rather on your chin or cheeks. Make sure to examine the effect in daylight. The right hue for you will barely (or not at all) differ from the rest of your skin. If you blush frequently or if your skin tends towards redness, you should use a yellowish foundation rather than a pinkish one.

FOUNDATION HINTS

- You can cover very dark patches of skin, for example sun or age marks, either by a second layer of foundation or by using a specific concealer. You should gently dab this on with your fingertips so as not to smudge the foundation.
- If you want to conceal rings under your eyes, it is best not to cover them completely, as this quickly looks unnatural.
- If bluish blood vessels shine through your eyelids, you can also tone these down with a bit of foundation.

There are a number of special anti-aging foundations available that contain moisturising substances which are gradually released so that the skin is supplied with adequate moisture throughout the day. They also contain reflecting pigments that make the lines of your face look softer and smoother.

Once you have found the most appropriate hue for your skin, it will be quite sufficient to only cover age-related blemishes, red patches and any burst blood vessels with a bit of foundation. Make sure to smudge over the edges carefully, so that the foundation blends naturally into the natural hue of your skin. Because wrinkles around your eyes and mouth do not differ in colour from the skin around them, there is really no need to cover them up.

POWDER

To give your make-up a professional finish, fix the foundation with some powder. Then nothing can smudge. Whether you prefer to use a transparent powder or one exactly matching your skin is entirely up to you. In either case, you should use powder very sparingly: it tends to settle down in wrinkles, thus emphasising them.

Many beauticians no longer apply powder with a brush or the good old fluffy powder puff, but swear by the new velours sponges that only take up a little powder. If you use a brush, you should dip it into the powder and then make sure to shake off the excess by gently knocking the brush against the edge of a table or washbasin before applying the powder to your face.

POWDER HINTS

- Loose powder can be more easily applied and can be used more sparingly.
- Put compacts in your handbag to freshen up your face throughout the day. This too, you should use sparingly.
- Always apply powder from top to bottom!
- If you find you have accidentally applied too much powder, remove the excess with a soft brush.

Powder and blusher brushes should be cleaned regularly, ideally once a month. Wash them gently in warm water with a mild shampoo. Then rinse them thoroughly under water, squeeze the water out and gently restore them to their original shape. Then place them onto a folded towel in such a way that the bristles protrude over an edge so that they can dry evenly from all sides.

Apply the foundation first.

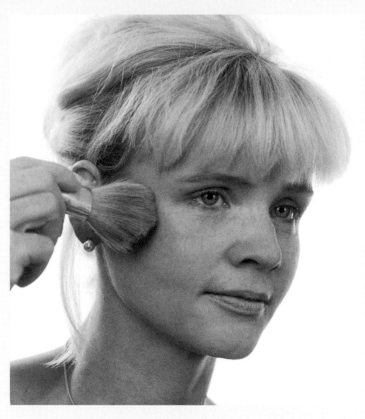

A little blusher will give your face a youthful look.

After treating your eyes, turn your attention to your lips.

Perfectly applied make-up has a natural appearance.

Blusher

A mere hint of blusher can miraculously create a touch of freshness, even in pale faces. Yet, here too, less is more. Round red cheeks can often seem unnatural, whereas a slight hint of rosiness will give your face a younger, healthier and more refreshed appearance. So make sure to thoroughly rid the brush of excess blusher before brushing it across your cheeks.

As long as your face is still nice and smooth, you can of course apply blusher to your cheekbones without a second thought. Purse your lips or simply say 'ooooh'. Your cheekbones will protrude, and you can then easily accentuate them with some blusher. There is some difference of opinion as to the direction in which the blusher should be applied: some people swear by strokes going from the inside diagonally upwards, whereas others recommend gentle swooping strokes from the ear towards the cheekbone. You should experiment to find out which method suits you best.

Once the first signs of advancing age become visible, it is important to adapt your blusher to match the changing contours of your face. If your cheeks have already sunk in a little, it could be rather more flattering to apply the blusher to the cheeks themselves. You will find just the right place to apply it by exaggerating a smile or grimace in the mirror. Gently apply some blusher to the part of your face that protrudes, and then continue until you reach the desired intensity. Clean the brush afterwards with a dry tissue and then blend the edges of the blusher in with your skin. Brownish hues tend to be more suitable for mature skin than bluish or reddish ones.

Blusher Hints

- To avoid looking 'painted', you should not apply the blusher until the end.
- Once you've applied the blusher, use a brush to smooth down the fine hairs on your cheeks in the direction of their growth. The effect is fascinating!
- A hint of blusher on your temples along the hairline will make your face look smoother; a bit on your chin rounds off your face.
- Cream blusher looks most natural if it is applied directly to the skin. That's why you should apply it after your moisturiser but before your powder.

EYE MAKE-UP

Successful eye make-up will give your eyes a brilliant sheen. You should take particular care when treating your eyes, since they are the highlight of your face.

First of all, you need to carefully prepare the region around your eyes: you can use a bit of foundation on the dark rings under your eyes, but don't try to cover them completely. Also, critically look at the inner corners of your eyes: the skin can quickly look darker here.

Chose colours from the same group for your eye make-up. You can even be a bit daring: your eye shadow doesn't necessarily have to have the same colour as your eyes. Brown eyes, for example, can look highly attractive with a smoky greyish purple. Slightly shiny eye shadow will make your eyes look bigger, but it shouldn't be too shiny and should be used sparingly.

If you don't like using traditional powder eye shadow, you could try the new creamy type. These preparations can be easily applied and spread with your fingertips and develop a nice, dull sheen. Powder eye shadow is best applied with a brush. Make sure to brush off any excess, so that you don't ruin the rest of your make-up with lose flakes. Avoid harsh transitions and always smudge the applied colour with the brush.

You will need a light, a medium and a dark colour for professional eye make-up. The light hue is applied to the brow bone, the medium one to your eyelid and the dark one is used to place highlights depending on the shape of your eye: if your eyes are set deep in the sockets, the dark

EYE MAKE-UP HINTS

- If you have wrinkly eyelids, you should avoid liquid eyeliners and use a soft pencil liner and smudge it with matching powder eye shadow.
- If you accidentally use too much eye shadow, you can neutralise this by pressing a well brushed-off facial powder sponge on your eyelids.
- To create a deep, emotional 'Bambi' look, only apply mascara to the outer half of your upper and lower lashes.

shade should be applied directly above the lashes, from the middle of the eyelid to the outer corner. If your eyes are almond-shaped, apply the dark shade above and below the eye: around the outside corner to the middle. Round eyes will appear narrower if you apply the dark shade in the outer third of the lower eyelid and move diagonally upwards past the outer corner of your eye. If your eyelids sag a little in the outer corner, emphasise the lower lid with the dark shade, and again extend it past the outer corner of your eye in an upward direction. In this case, you should also only apply mascara to the outer third of your upper lashes. Finally, if you have drooping eyelids, you should only apply the light shade to the upper and lower lids and use the medium shade to accentuate the fold.

Mascara 'opens' your eyes and makes them look larger. You can even intensify this effect by applying a dark powder eye shadow with a damp eyeliner brush – this looks milder than eyeliner. Mascara should always enhance a natural look and not a painted one. Black mascara can form a harsh contrast to your paling complexion; in this case, changing to brown mascara will have a more flattering effect.

Make sure that your lashes don't stick together and that your mascara doesn't leave lumps. Such 'fly-legs' are enough to ruin any make-up. Clean your mascara brush before using it with a paper tissue, and replace your mascara every three months. Exercise care when using water-resistant mascara. Firstly, it can dry out your eyelashes; and secondly, it is difficult to remove, and make-up remains are highly detrimental to the delicate and sensitive skin around your eyes.

Your Eyebrows

Just like a portrait that develops its full potential in a matching frame, your eyes can benefit from well-groomed eyebrows. The narrow strips of hair above your eyes not only protect them from perspiration and dirt, but ideally add shape and expression to your face. Have you ever noticed how 'naked' Mona Lisa's face seems? This is because her eyebrows, in accordance with the fashion of the time, were radically plucked and barely visible.

Perfectly shaped brows, on the other hand, can visually balance out the increasingly slackening area around your eyes and give your whole face a younger appearance. Emphasise the natural bow of your brows.

The highest point should be above your iris when you are looking straight ahead. Your brows should begin above the inner corner of your eyes and sweep as far out as possible.

Your eyebrows should not dominate your face, but rather form a beautiful frame for your eyes. And that's why they should only be highlighted with caution: dark, massive beam-like brows not only look unnatural, but also make your whole face seem mask-like and sinister. Define them subtly with an eyebrow pencil or a powder eye shadow. You will achieve a particularly natural look if you accentuate your brows with two different but matching hues.

If you only want to define your brows a little, it is quite sufficient to use a small hard brush to apply a some eyebrow powder or eye shadow to the hairs and then brush them into shape. If, however, you have small gaps to fill, you might want to proceed in the following, more complex way: brush the hairs of your eyebrows downwards with a small, dry brush. Then gently draw the missing hairs onto your skin with a soft eyebrow pencil. After that, apply some eye shadow to the entire brow – this will perfectly hide the transition between the drawn and the real hairs. Finally, brush your eyebrows into shape again carefully.

If you want to pluck your eyebrows, you can outline the perfect shape with an eyebrow liner and then remove the hairs that do not fit in. Be very cautious while plucking and constantly check the result in the mirror so that you don't remove too many hairs or create little gaps. Always work

Very dark eyebrows look far too harsh in combination with light, highlighted or grey hair. A lighter hue, such as a light smoky blue, is much more flattering. Red-haired women should be cautious of all reddish hues – these can often look unnatural.

EYEBROW HINTS

- You can easily tame unruly eyebrows by spraying some hairspray onto a little brush and then shaping your eyebrows with it.

Plucking eyebrows is less painful

- if you use good tweezers;
- if you pluck the hairs in the direction of growth;
- if you stretch the skin around the hairs with your fingers;
- if you rub an ice cube across your eyebrows before plucking them.

on both eyes alternately, moving away from the nose, so that you get an even result. If you are not sure about the right contour, you can have your eyebrows plucked into shape professionally by a beautician, and then all you have to do is neaten them up occasionally.

LIPSTICK

Perfectly applied lipstick in a flattering colour can make your whole face look years younger; no wonder lipstick is one of the most popular beauty utensils and a lot of women feel somehow 'naked' without it.

Natural, subtle colours are often more flattering than dark or very bright ones. A lot of perfumeries and drugstores now have colour palettes with which it is an easy matter to find the colour and hue that best suits your complexion. The older we get, the more likely our lipstick is to change its colour after application. That's why you had best test the lipstick to see if it will continue to look good on your lips.

Because our lips gradually become drier as we age, wrinkles are likely to settle around our mouth fairly quickly and lipstick tends to run into them.

Long-lasting lipsticks are very practical but, depending on their composition, can strongly dehydrate the sensitive skin on your lips. If you suffer from dry lips anyway, it is best to touch up your lip make-up throughout the day or evening.

LIPSTICK HINTS

- If you want to give your lips a fuller appearance, apply the outliner just beyond the natural line of your lips, then blur it towards the inside without smudging it. Then apply your lipstick.
- To softly define the outline of your mouth, run the outliner across the back of your hand a couple of times. It will then get a rounder, softer tip.
- If your lips are so wrinkly that you have difficulty applying lipstick, you should stretch them between the forefinger and middle finger of one hand, while using the other to apply the lipstick.
- Treat yellowish shades with caution: they can easily make your teeth look yellow and unpleasant. If in doubt, red shades are more flattering.

If your lips are often very dry or rough you should pamper them regularly with a generous layer of lip balm, which you should leave to sink in for at least five minutes.

To avoid the embarassment of running lipstick, beauticians recommend that you first put foundation on your lips or powder them, then use an outliner and finally apply the lipstick with a special brush. Make sure the colour of your outliner corresponds to your lipstick or to the natural colour of your lips.

You should only use a little lip gloss to accentuate the middle of your lips, since it is so runny that it might settle in the tiny wrinkles around your mouth. More lasting highlights can be achieved by using glossy lipsticks: a little bit applied to the middle of the upper and lower lip are often more effective than a completely glossy mouth.

PERFUME

A good perfume can help lift your spirits and make you feel completely beautiful and well-groomed. In order to enjoy your valuable essences to the full, however, you should pay attention to a few points.

Some women put their perfume behind their ears – but often the skin there is so oily that it doesn't carry the scent properly.

If you would like to go out into the sun, you should be cautious with using perfume: depending on how sensitive your skin is, the perfume can cause it to acquire a permanent brownish colour in the places where you apply it. That's why you should best avoid combining perfume with a sunbath, or bend your head forward and apply a little of the scent to the bottom of your hair.

Less is also more when it comes to perfume. Especially if you have been using one and the same scent for several years, you won't be able to smell it so well yourself and will tend to adopt an inflationary approach, using it in ever-increasing amounts. For your surroundings, there tends to be a smooth transition between a subtle scent and an irritating odour. Especially with very intensive scents, it is often sufficient to spray some into the air and then walk through it, or to only spray a little onto your hair. If you prefer to wear it on your skin, a tiny (!) drop each on the inside of your wrists, in the back of your knees, on the back of your neck and between your breasts is quite sufficient.

Our skin changes with progressing age, especially during menopause. This can result in your favourite perfume suddenly developing a different scent from the one you have become used to. Sometimes the scent suddenly becomes unpleasant for your friends or you no longer like it yourself. If you still don't want to go without your favourite perfume, you could try the following tricks: put some drops of perfume either onto one or more handkerchiefs or into unglazed clay pots, and distribute these in your wardrobe. Your clothes will absorb the scent, and you will smell good without wearing it directly on your skin. You could also try applying the perfume directly to your clothes, but you should try this on a seam first. If this works, the best places to put the perfume are under the collar, on the hem and on your cuffs.

YOUR HAIR

We all hate waking up and looking into the mirror only to discover that it's going to be a 'bad hair day' – one of those days where our hair simply refuses to do what we want it to. Often we feel so uncomfortable about ourselves on such days that a lot of other things go pear-shaped as well… Of course, it's best to not let it even get that far! An attractive, suitable hairstyle that goes along with the natural growth of your hair and which you can easily handle has a considerable effect on your well-being, thereby also contributing to your self-confidence and charisma.

Nowadays, there is such a broad variety of hairstyles on offer that you can quite easily find a suitable one for any personality, face contour and age group. Forget the general rule that a short haircut is the only one that comes into consideration for older women, especially when their hair starts to turn grey. Fashion has changed fundamentally! As long as your hairstyle matches your personality and your age, you can wear your hair any way you like.

Most hairstyles are based on variety. Chin-length to shoulder-length hair can be styled in a particular variety, especially if your hair is long enough for a pony tail or to be pinned up. And don't let yourself be talked into a practical short haircut if you prefer longer hair yourself. Nowadays, there are so many good conditioning products available that even hip-length hair can look shiny and buoyant with the appropriate care, rather than limp and dull.

Although a short haircut is practical and easy to look after, it can also look very stern and harsh. Short hair looks best if you have a nicely shaped head or shapely ears. But if you want to hide some feature (e.g. a flat skull or big ears) with your hair, slightly longer hair might be better for you.

Whatever the hairstyle, the most important consideration is the actual cut. If you've had one and the same haircut for several years, you might want to critically scrutinise yourself and see if it still suits you and your personality. Would any of us want to look like the photo on our first job application for the rest of our lives? If you have tried out various hairstyles and lengths, get out the photos and look at them. Which of them do you like best on yourself? Can you remember whether your hair could be easily styled with this haircut?

Flip through magazines or hair-specials every once in a while to find out which styles and cuts you like best. This will help you to determine your favourite haircut. Take the photos on which you like your hair best along to your next appointment at the hairdresser's. That should make it easier to explain what you want to the stylist, and they can tell you if your hair is suitable for this.

Some hair salons now offer a special service: you can sit down in front of a camera and your image is directly transferred to a computer. Together with your stylist you can run through several simulations and see what you would look like with various hairstyles on the screen.

If your hairdresser advises you against your dream style, ask him or her to explain the reasons in detail. The reason could be the structure of your hair, or that the haircut doesn't match the shape of your face, or maybe that it is so complicated to style properly that you wouldn't be able to do it by yourself. In such a case, ask the specialist to show you alternatives – ideally on pictures or your photos. If you just can't make up your mind on the spot, you should arrange a new appointment rather than being talked into a particular hairstyle.

Before setting off to the hairdresser, dress and apply your make-up no differently from the way you would any other day. This will give a realistic impression of yourself. If you prefer wearing jeans and sweaters and do a lot of exercise, you will probably need a completely different haircut from someone your age who mostly wears suits and goes on a lot of business trips. The ideal hairstyle will combine your dream with an easy-to-handle, uncomplicated haircut that provides a great styling variety. And if your hair can be styled in a number of different ways, you can soon get the better of a 'bad hair day'.

Perfectly groomed long hair can often be worn open or in a simple pony tail, in a classic bun or can be seductively pinned up. Chin-length to shoulder-length hair can look different with a new parting, can be put up in a pony tail, decorated with a bow that matches your wardrobe, can be pinned up or kept back with a scarf. It can also be simply combed back with some gel or styling mousse. A well conceived, perfectly cut short haircut with slightly longer hair on top can also be restyled quite quickly and easily: a little wax can be used to make it look spiky, mousse and a diffuser will turn it into a mop of curly hair, it can be elegantly held back from your face with an attractive scarf or made to look as if you've just stepped out of a time machine from the twenties, with a lot of gel and a stern parting.

It is important that the basic haircut suits the contours of your face. If you are not too sure what shape your face has, tie your hair back and stand in front of a mirror topless. Close one eye, and trace the outline of your face from your hairline to your chin onto the mirror with a soft eyeliner (this can be easily removed with window cleaner). Then add ears, neck and the top of your head. What does the shape look like? Is it a regular oval, or more of an upright rectangle? Is it square? Does it look a triangle standing on its tip with a broad forehead and a pointed chin? Or the opposite with your chin being the broadest part of your face?

Your haircut should match the contours of your face. Since your face tends to become narrower as you age, you should occasionally check whether the shape of your face has changed and perhaps adapt your hairstyle accordingly. More mature faces, which show lines and wrinkles more clearly, benefit from full, flowing hair.

Hair Conditioning Hints

Pollution and blow-drying your hair at too hot a setting strain your hair, which is additionally getting thinner and often more fragile with age. That's why you should pay more attention to your hair once you reach forty.

- Have the ends of your hair trimmed regularly.
- Pamper it regularly by using a conditioner that is suitable for your hair. Don't over-condition your hair, otherwise it will become limp and can't be styled so well any longer.
- Avoid blow-drying your hair for too long and at too hot a setting. Dry it with a towel or let it dry naturally, and only use your hair-dryer for styling purposes.
- If your hair becomes static, either put some hairspray onto your hands or breathe into your hands and then run them through your hair, or use a conditioner that is not rinsed out.

For more body:

- Blow-dry your hair upside down, i.e. the 'wrong' way, and keep ruffling up the roots.
- Good old curlers have become fashionable again: you can now get ones that are easy to handle and that will add some body to your hair when applied at the roots.
- Fine hair should be washed daily, and ideally with a body-enhancing shampoo.

If you've been blessed with an even oval face, you can wear basically whatever hairstyle you like. Longish faces are made to look even longer by straight hair that is parted in the middle. For this shape, chin-length styles with full sides, asymmetric partings and/or a fringe are the most suitable. Faces that have a square shape are best suited by fullness on the top of the head, which gives an elongated impression. Longer hair should be tapered at the sides, and shorter hair pulled back behind the ears. If you have a rather broad forehead and a pointed chin, the classic 'page-boy' style might suit you best: the hair is cut off just below the ears, with the fringe slightly tapered. A triangular face with a broad chin and a high forehead is best framed by full sides and top. A slightly tapered, asymmetrical fringe will appear to reduce the size of your forehead. If your forehead is full of wrinkles already, a fluffy fringe or a few strands of hair can nicely hide this.

GREY HAIR

A lot of women get their first grey hairs in the middle of their twenties, and after their thirty-fifth birthday these generally increase in number. Grey hair lacks the colorant melanin. It tend to be thicker and more stubborn than your original hair and generally is less shiny because it is lacking the colour pigments that reflect light. In addition, a face surrounded by grey hair tends to look pale and older, although there are some women who in fact look highly attractive with grey hair. These women mostly have either very light skin or very dark hair. However, a lot of women feel uncomfortable with grey hair. What can be done?

Plucking your hairs is useless: hairs with the original colour will no longer grow in their place. If you are very unsatisfied with your grey hair, all you can do is to dye it. However, you should pay attention to the following: for your hair to look natural, you should only change from your current colour by a few shades and avoid strong contrasts. Blond women should avoid ash-blond hues and go for golden hues or highlights so as not to look too pale. Brunettes or dark-haired women should always use a dye that is one to two shades lighter than their original colour and maybe even use highlights for additional shine. Hair that is too dark contrasts too much with the pale skin, looks unnatural and will make you look older than you really are. Before completely dyeing your hair, you should also consider covering up the 'damage' with less drastic methods.

If you are blond and have only a few grey hairs, you could perhaps hide these with highlighted strands. Highlights have to be redone about every eight to twelve weeks. If you have darker hair, a good stylist can dye the grey hairs with your original hair colour. You could also use a colouring shampoo or conditioner.

If your grey hairs start to increase in number, non-permanent colorants or dyes can be helpful. These products envelop each hair with a thin coating of colour without damaging it. The colour mixes with the grey hue and therefore looks very natural. Non-permanent colorants are rinsed out after several washes.

The next longer lasting colorant is semi-permanent dye. It lasts much longer than a non-permanent one, because it opens up the scaly layer of each individual hair and reaches the core. When you use permanent hair dyes, they even reach the roots of your hair, so that you will have to re-dye the roots every four to six weeks.

NATURAL RECIPES FOR COPING WITH GREY HAIR

You can quite easily make some simple and effective products to control stubborn grey hair yourself.

Conditioner for sheen
Boil up three tablespoons of saponaria in $^3/_4$ litre (1$^1/_2$ pints) of water. Add three tablespoons of orange juice, three egg yolks and four drops of orange oil. Mix thoroughly and let stew for 10 minutes. Then pour the mixture into bottles.

Strengthening conditioner with lavender vinegar
Put a tablespoon each of lavender blossoms and birch leaves into a bottle and add a litre (2 pints) of cider vinegar. Leave for a week and then strain through a sieve. To use this mixture, blend one part of lavender vinegar with two parts of water. Massage into your hair thoroughly and do not rinse out.

Conditioner for stubborn, dry hair
Mash the pulp of half an avocado and mix it with an egg yolk and a teaspoon of jojoba oil. Put the paste onto your hair and leave for 15 minutes. Then rinse out and wash your hair with a mild shampoo.

Hair dyes and colorants are often suspected of irritating your skin, damaging your hair and possibly even increasing the risk of cancer, so always test the product on the inside of your elbow to see whether you are allergic to it, and protect your skin and hands from direct contact with the product. Avoid using a colorant or dye if your scalp is irritated or if you have small cuts on it. If you dye your hair yourself, make sure that you adhere to the time limit given and that you thoroughly rinse out the colour in time. You shouldn't colour your hair too often; you can also hide grown-out roots with hair mascara.

If you are at peace with your grey strands or hair, you can do a lot for your appearance with a few simple tricks. For example, if your hair turns grey at a relatively early age you can adopt a playful approach to the contrast between your youthful face and 'old' hair. This can be especially attractive when combined with an attractive haircut. The contrast can be emphasised by make-up using subtle, natural colours. As a general rule, you should use subtle colours to avoid the impression of paleness caused by grey or white hair.

Not only grey hair, but in fact all types of mature hair call for a specific care programme. Once you reach menopause, you will find that the structure of your hair starts to change: it has less pigmentation, and your hair loses body. A healthy blood circulation in your scalp is absolutely necessary for your hair to be constantly supplied with everything it needs to stay healthy and beautiful. Your diet also plays a role in this: vitamins, minerals and trace elements are important for giving your hair 'body' and structure. Any deficiencies will become plainly visible: you hair will become dull, limp and brittle.

Just how strong and robust your hair is also depends on some external factors: too much sun, environmental influence and straining chemical treatments will have negative effects. Consistent care and cleansing can help prevent this.

How to Prevent Hair Loss

A lot of women's hair thins as they age. Often this is simply an unavoidable result of aging. Sometimes, however, hair loss – especially when it occurs suddenly – has a more serious cause. If you have noticed the following symptoms for quite some time, you should try to determine the cause:

- You lose significantly more hair when washing or brushing it.

- Your parting is getting wider.

- You notice more and more short hairs at the roots.

- When you pull your hair back to a pony tail, this is significantly thinner than it used to be.

There are many reasons for hair loss: sometimes it is hereditary. But the hormonal changes during menopause can also make hair loss a women's problem. It could, however, be a side-effect of some medication or of hormone replacement therapy, and it could be caused by a deficiency of nutrients, e.g. iron. Other possible causes are stress, lack of sleep, inappropriate care, or external damage caused by hot blow-drying or aggressive dyes. Consulting a doctor might provide you with an answer.

Whereas we still can't do anything to prevent hereditary hair loss, hair problems related to menopause are often only a transitory occurrence.

As preventive measures you could try to provide your hair with the appropriate nutrients through a healthy diet or to stimulate the blood circulation of your scalp by exercise or regular scalp massages. You don't need a highly specific method: simply massage your scalp from front to back every day, with small circular movements. Then grab your hair as though you wanted to pull it out; but make sure you don't pull too strongly.

Beauty Treatment for Your Hands

The neck and hands are telltale indicators of a woman's true age. To reduce this 'betrayal' to a minimum, you should look after your hands and be sure to give them some special care.

The skin of our hands is exposed to a variety of stress factors throughout the day: they are often exposed to the sun without protection and have to deal with frequent washing as well as aggressive detergents and cleaning products. This is why you should carry a tube of hand cream with you at all times (ideally one with a sun protection factor) and use it whenever your hands are subjected to stressful conditions.

Regular exercise keeps your hands supple and elastic. Fold your hands and then stretch your arms away from you at chest height. The palms of your hands should be facing away from you. Hold this tension for half a minute and then release it. Let your arms hang by your side and then slowly lift them to shoulder height. While doing this, move your hands backwards and forwards from the wrists. Slowly lower your arms again, but keep moving your hands. Drum on the table with your fingertips

Hand Care Hints

- Always use a mild soap for washing your hands.
- Regularly moisturise your hands.
- Exfoliate your hands regularly (e.g. with a mixture of oil and salt) and then pamper them with a cream pack.
- Every now and then, you should treat your hands with a night cream that you allow to sink in overnight (while wearing cotton gloves). Massage the remaining cream into your hands the next morning.

occasionally: this stimulates the blood circulation. You can also get massaging balls, which you kneed with your hands.

A good manicure will immediately give your hands a well-kept appearance. Soften your nails with some warm water and oil and cut them. Gently press back the cuticles. If you file your nails, work from the edges to the middle and in one direction only.

Nail polish can provide a good protective layer for brittle nails. Chose a colour that flatters the skin colour of your hands. Very bright and very pale colours will make your hands look pallid and grey. Extremely long red 'claws' aren't very flattering for older women – shorter nails and a French manicure with white edges are more natural and more elegant. When you paint your nails, first apply a clear base coat, then apply two coats of coloured polish and finish off with a clear protective top coat. This will make the polish last much longer and you will spare your nails the strain of removing the polish. Use a gentle polish remover without acetone to prevent your nails from drying out and becoming brittle.

You should regularly examine your nails. If you notice any obvious changes, you should consult a doctor: if they become thicker, look milky or suddenly become brittle, this could be caused by a nail fungus. Spotty nails are sometimes a sign of psoriasis, and a dark discolouring under your nail can even be a sign of cancer.

WELL-KEPT FEET

Are you up and about a lot? Then it shouldn't really surprise you if your feet start showing the first signs of fatigue and wear after giving you several decades of faithful service.

Since our feet carry our entire weight, they become wider in the course of our lifetime. And since the instep can also sink as the years go by, your feet might become bigger by half or a whole size. Keep a regular check on your shoe size so as not to torture your feet with shoes that are too small or too tight.

It is best to try on new shoes in the afternoon: in the morning, your feet are still relaxed and tend to be narrower.

Rest your legs every now and then and put them up: this will help prevent swelling and water retention in your feet and legs. Brisk walks will get your circulation going and are a good way of preventing cold feet. Try not to cross your legs: this cuts off the circulation and can cause premature varicose veins and hair veins (a profusion of minute veins directly below the surface of the skin on your legs that shine through the skin like a bluish net). If your feet hurt when you walk, you might want to consider using medical insoles.

The skin on your feet is quite dry in any case and will become even drier as you age. To avoid chapping and infections, you should pamper your feet with some additional care: rub some rich cream or warm olive oil into them after your evening foot bath. Then put on cotton socks and allow the oils to sink in overnight. Massage the remaining oil or cream into your feet with gentle circular movements in the morning. A standard body moisturiser is often not sufficient for your tired feet; in this case, you should select a special moisturising foot lotion.

If you would like to spoil yourself and your feet, you should treat yourself to a pedicure every ten to twelve weeks. Alternatively, you can pamper your feet yourself with the following routine: soak them in hot water for five minutes to soften the skin and nails; cut your nails and file down the corners. Cut them off straight and not round, otherwise you could get ingrown toenails. Then gently push back the cuticles, and use a mild exfoliator or a loofah glove to remove the dead skin flakes. When using your pumice stone to remove callous skin, take care not to remove too much. Finally, massage a rich but not too oily cream into your feet.

Regularly examine your feet for ingrown toenails, corns and fungal infections so that these can be treated as soon as possible. If you notice eczema or other significant changes to the skin on your feet or legs, you should consult a dermatologist.

Foot Care Hints

- Remove callous skin from dry feet – if they swell up after being soaked in the bath for a long time, there is a danger of removing too much.
- Peppermint gets tired feet moving again. Bathe them in a peppermint tea for 15 minutes and then put a generous amount of cream on them.
- Can you pick up a pencil with your toes? If not: practise doing this. And try walking on your toes more often – this will keep your feet supple. You can also press the soles of your feet against a wall, and 'climb' up it with your toes. Another good exercise for your feet is to stand on your toes and then slowly roll your feet back onto their heels.

You feet will also be grateful if you put on clean socks every day, walk barefoot frequently – not only in summer! – and often change the height of your heels.

Healthy, Beautiful Teeth

A beautiful smile with healthy teeth is an extremely attractive sight to behold. Cleaning your teeth thoroughly and properly is not just part of a beauty programme but is also beneficial to your health.

Regular check-ups at the dentist are just as important as brushing them daily. After your fortieth birthday, you should visit the dentist two to four times a year. Regularly have the tartar removed and your teeth polished. Apart from toothache, there are further alarm signals such as a sudden onset of bad breath or an unpleasant taste in your mouth that should make you consult your dentist immediately so that the cause can be determined.

Brushing your teeth – ideally three times a day after your meals – should be part of your standard tooth care programme. Ask your dentist for advice on which kind of toothbrush is the most suitable for you. Nowadays, a lot of tooth hygiene specialists also work in dental practices and they can show you how to use dental floss, inter-dental sticks and brushes. Only thorough tooth hygiene can prevent plaque, which serves as an ideal breeding ground for caries and other infections of the mouth. A first sign

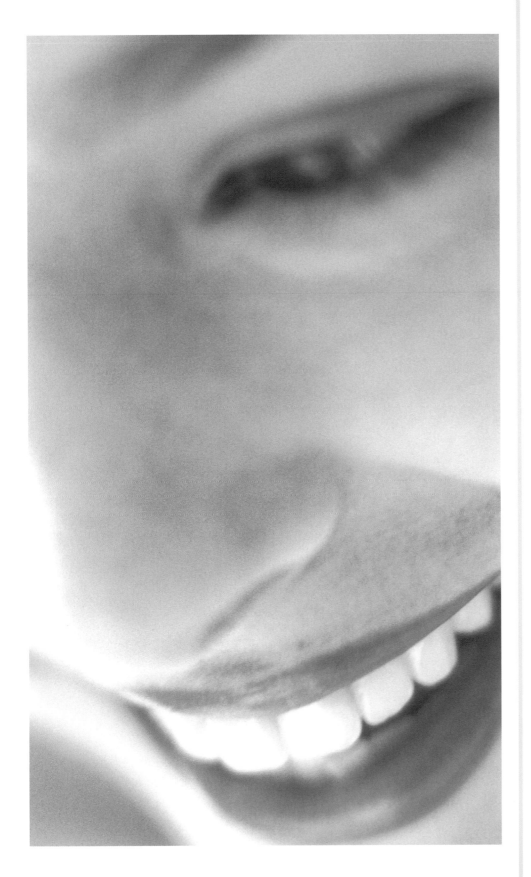

For reasons of hygiene, you should change your toothbrush every month. Nowadays, there are several environment-friendly toothbrushes available with disposable heads.

of plaque is bleeding of the gums while brushing your teeth. If you notice this, you should go to your dentist – otherwise you will risk gum infection and deterioration.

A sensible and balanced diet is very important for healthy teeth. What a lot of people don't know, however, is that too much sugar but also too much stress can change the conditions in your mouth to such an extent that the risk of tooth and gum infections increases. If you like chewing gum, chose sugar-free varieties. These stimulate the production of saliva just as much as chewing gum containing sugar but are not as detrimental to your teeth. And if you are prone to gum infections, rinse your mouth with hot sage tea after brushing your teeth – this has a disinfectant and anti-inflammatory effect.

To keep your teeth a glowing white, you should ideally give up smoking. Excessive consumption of tea and coffee also has a discolouring effect. But don't experiment with bleaching products – seek advice from your dentist if you are not satisfied with the colour of your teeth.

Treatment in the Beauty Salon

Beauticians and beauty farms offer a variety of treatments that promise improved, more youthful looks. As a supplement to your daily care programme, such 'extras' can be beneficial and sensible – but they can neither replace your daily care nor can they work wonders.

For each type of treatment you should make sure that you entrust yourself to the care of well-trained and experienced professionals. Improper treatment can leave lasting damage that virtually disfigures you. Also, take a close look at the salon: does it give a clean, hygienic impression?

Superficial treatment such as facial massages and masks, or vaporisation, in which a fine film of water is sprayed onto your skin, only has a limited effect on the surface of your skin. Very small creases can be temporarily straightened out, but they won't disappear completely. You should avoid steam treatment, especially if you have mature skin, because it can cause blood vessels to burst.

If you have very sensitive skin, insist on masks or creams are tested in inconspicuous places first. The older you are, the less often you should use facial masks. If you do, make sure that they are moisturising masks. Do you suffer from acne, spots, eczema, an acute infection (e.g. coldsores), or do you tend to get burst blood vessels? Then you had better go without a mask. The same applies to exfoliation.

Exfoliation, in which special acids are applied to your skin, interferes with its natural balance. If you have very sensitive skin, you should go without them or have them tested in an inconspicuous place before allowing the product to be applied to your face.

Professional lymphatic drainage can visibly freshen up an exhausted face. If you suffer from cancer, a heart disorder, thrombosis or risk of embolism, such treatments are out of the question for you. You need to be especially cautious if you suffer from asthma, low blood pressure or have already had thrombosis. Make sure you point this out to the professional.

Nowadays, various versions of laser therapy are also used in beauty treatment: the range goes from sclerosing spider veins to permanently removing undesired body hair. It is especially important to only allow well-trained professionals to carry out this treatment on you. If you have any doubts about their qualifications, you had best go without this treatment. Find out if they are sufficiently insured, too. Dermabrasion of the skin is particularly effective in evening out acne scars or wrinkles around the mouth. However, this should only be carried out by an experienced dermatologist or plastic surgeon.

MENOPAUSE – AN END AND A NEW START

The menopause marks a significant change in a woman's life: the transition from being fertile to no longer being able to reproduce. Physical complaints can go along with this transformation, but many women primarily suffer from the psychological aspects of the menopause: they fear old age or a feeling of emptiness once their children have moved out from home. However, you will suffer much less from the unpleasant symptoms if you prepare yourself mentally and physically for the menopause: regard this transitional period as the beginning of a new life phase.

A Change, a Transition, a New Start...

Nowadays, it is hard to imagine that until well into the 19th century, a woman's life expectancy more or less coincided with the onset of menopause. The common view was that once women stopped having periods, their glands started to change and they ran the risk of going insane. Today, we know much more about the highly complex processes within the female body and have realised that the phenomenon of menopause is closely related to the female hormone balance.

During menopause, the body gradually stops producing the hormones progesterone and oestrogen. These hormones primarily regulate fertility, but are also important for a quite number of other processes, such as metabolism for example. The hormone deficiency caused by the menopause is the cause of a lot of the physical ailment that arise during this time of a woman's life.

The menstrual cycle is jointly controlled by the brain and the ovaries. Menopause begins when the functionality of the ovaries is exhausted.

How Oestrogen and Progesterone Control the Menstrual Cycle

The menstrual cycle is determined by highly complex processes in the body. At the beginning of the cycle, the cerebrum sends out a signal within the brain to the hypothalamus telling it to release the hormone FSH. This hormone then causes ova (eggs) to mature in the ovaries. In response to this, some follicles grow in the ovaries and simultaneously produce the hormone oestrogen, which causes the endometrium (the lining of the uterus) to thicken, in order to prepare the uterus for fertilisation. Once a certain concentration of oestrogen is present in the blood, the cerebrum makes the hypothalamus release the hormone LH, which causes ovulation. One ripe ovum is released from the follicle, makes its way through the fallopian tube and then makes its way towards the uterus. The follicle then turns into yellow tissue known as corpus luteum and starts secreting the hormone progesterone. This stops the endometrium from thickening further, stimulates it instead to absorb nutrients. If a fertilised egg is not implanted within a specific time, the corpus luteum dies. The hormone level in the blood diminishes and menstruation starts. After this, a new cycle begins.

The brain continues to send out commands in the form of hormones, but the ovaries no longer respond. How this complicated control mechanism works is explained in the box on the facing page.

By the time you have had your last period – which in our cultural environment is mostly in your early fifties – you are already right in the middle of the menopause. That's why you shouldn't worry if you are suffering from menopausal complaints and are still having your periods. Long before the last period, your body starts reducing its hormone production. Menopause starts when your hormone production is diminished and stops when your body has become used to the new hormone balance. This normally takes about ten years; with some women it can take longer.

CLIMACTERIC AND MENOPAUSE – WHAT IS THE DIFFERENCE?

You will come across a variety of terms concerning the menopause in different books and magazines. This has to do with the fact that from a medical perspective, this period can be divided into individual phases. In the table on the following page, the most important terms have been compiled and are explained briefly.

Normally, you will find that your menstrual cycle is irregular for quite some time before your periods stop for good. You no longer have your periods at regular four-week intervals, and frequently they are either stronger or weaker than they used to be. A lot of women get pregnant during this time before the menopause, because they wrongly assume that they are no longer fertile. But you can only be sure that menopause has taken place if you haven't had a period for over a year. That's why contraception can still be an important consideration during the time before menopause.

Women who smoke, are underweight or have either had no children or twins often reach the menopause a lot sooner, sometimes even before the age of 40. The surgical removal of the ovaries also expedites the onset of menopause. If you are over 55 and are still having periods, your doctor should determine the cause of this. Your menstrual cycle might still be working properly; however, growths in the uterus can also cause bleeding and can become malignant. If your menopause doesn't start until well

Some Important Terms

What?	When?
The **Climacteric** refers to the entire time span, i.e. the transition between the ovaries' full functionality and their complete standstill.	mostly between the age of 45 and 55
The last period in a woman's life to be triggered by the ovaries is called **Menopause**. This can only be precisely determined afterwards, when there has been no period for at least a year.	around the age of 50
Pre-Menopause is the time leading up to the last period, when periods are already becoming irregular.	mostly between the age of 45 and 50
The ten years after the last period are called **Post-Menopause**.	depends on the time of menopause
The time span one to two years before and after the last period is the **Peri-Menopause.**	depends on the time of menopause

after your 50th birthday, there is an increased risk of developing cancer of the uterus or breast cancer.

How a Woman's Body Changes during Menopause

If you want to know when your menopause begins and what it will be like, just ask your mother. Mostly, menopause is very similar between mothers and daughters.

A change of hormone level is typical of the menopause, and it can be accompanied by a variety of complaints. The course taken by menopause and the extent to which it is perceived as burdensome vary significantly from one woman to the next. Whereas some women only notice an irregularity and then an absence of their periods, others suffer from a variety of partly annoying, partly unpleasant symptoms that considerably affect their general condition.

Generally speaking, however, menopause is not a disease, but a natural process. A number of the complaints attributed to menopause disappear again once the body has become used to the change in hormones. Hot flushes and sweating, for example, tend to stop occurring once you've had your last period. The same is often true of psychological symptoms such as depression and listlessness.

Regular screening tests are recommended to diagnose cancer at an early stage. Apart from that, though, medical treatment during the menopause is only necessary if you are feeling very poorly or are suffering from exceptional complaints. You should, for example, definitely consult a doctor if you start bleeding years after your period has stopped even though you haven't been treated with hormones. This could perhaps be an indication of cancer.

Once your ovaries cease to function, your brain stimulates your adrenal glands and fatty tissue to significantly increase their production of oestrogen. But on the whole the oestrogen level is drastically reduced. Actually, the generic term 'oestrogen' refers to quite a number of different hormones, which not only regulate the female reproductive system but also have other important functions within the body: for example, they influence the growth of body cells and bones, contribute to processes in the digestive system, stimulate the blood circulation and protect against hardening of the arteries. Oestrogen also regulates the retention of water in the skin.

At the beginning of menopause, a lot of women suffer from irregular, sometimes painful periods of varying length and intensity. Headaches are also very frequent. A lot of women suffer from weight gain or redistribution of fat during the menopause. Blood pressure and cholesterol levels can increase.

The oestrogen deficiency also disturbs the calcium balance within the female body. Quite a number of women complain of backaches and pains in their arms and legs. The danger of bone fractures increases with age because the balance of minerals in the skeleton is gradually reduced and after the menopause, osteoporosis leads to a marked reduction in bone density.

Most partners and relatives have a lack of understanding for psychological problems such as depression, melancholy, increased nervous tension and irritability or occasional memory weaknesses which can also occur during menopause. Frequently, sleeping patterns change too. Some women complain of sleeping disorders or are woken by night sweats, so that they feel tired and exhausted the next day.

Various factors influence the intensity and length of hot flushes: They can, for example, be caused by alcohol, coffee, or stress and excitement. Very slim women and those who don't sweat a lot frequently suffer more from hot flushes. Smoking narrows the vessels, thereby prolonging the hot flush.

The feared hot flushes that a lot of women suffer from during menopause are caused by the sinking levels of oestrogen in the body. The hormone deficiency disrupts the body's heat-regulating system. That's why the body temperature can suddenly plummet.

The body's autonomic nervous system tries to compensate for this heat loss: the blood vessels widen and emit more heat; at the same time, the stress hormone adrenaline is released. Women going through menopause experience this process as a sudden, intense and mostly rising heat rush in the upper half of their body. Frequently, the skin reddens and some women suffer from headaches and palpitations. A hot flush normally lasts about three to six minutes. Especially at the beginning of menopause, quite a lot of women have several hot flushes per hour which are then frequently followed by heavy sweating. Afterwards, a lot of women feel very cold. These hot flushes can sometimes be very unpleasant, but they are not dangerous.

A woman's body contains not only female, but also a certain amount of male hormones. When the female ones are diminished during menopause, the male ones become more dominant. This can lead to hair weakening and thinning. First signals are that your hair doesn't keep its shape. On the other hand, you will suddenly find hair growing in places where you consider it a nuisance – for example facial hair. In very slim women, even a slight increase of weight can be of benefit, because body fat can partly transform male hormones into oestrogen.

Around this time, your skin also starts to age more quickly. Young people's skin can retain a lot of water, which is why it looks firm and healthy. But even from the mid-thirties on, your skin starts to become thinner and drier, and once you reach menopause and your oestrogen level sinks, the skin's water balance is disrupted even more. Your skin gets drier, becomes more sensitive to outer stimulants and occasionally becomes taut or even starts flaking.

During menopause, a lot of women's mucous membranes become thinner and drier – also a result of the reduction in oestrogen levels. The symptoms are, for example, a dry mouth or very dry nose, but can also include problems during intercourse. The eyes tend to be dry, and some women can no longer tolerate wearing contact lenses. Occasionally, women suffer from frequent bleeding of the gums.

Your hair and skin also change during menopause. A lot of women can suddenly no longer tolerate the lotions they have been using up to this time and need a new type of body and face care. If you are uncertain about what your skin needs now, simply ask your dermatologist or pharmacist. When your hair begins to thin out, the first grey hairs show even more. A new, perhaps trendy hairstyle can work miracles. Highlighted strands of hair hide grey hairs and makes it more voluminous. Very intense colours can quickly have a harsh effect when contrasting with your skin, which is now getting paler.

In connection with menopause, you have to expect an increased loss of bone density – 'osteoporosis'. The susceptibility to cardiovascular diseases, which – up until menopause – women are protected against to a certain degree by their body's oestrogen production, also increases.

MAINTAINING PSYCHOLOGICAL STABILITY

Thanks to medical progress, more and more people reach a high age in fairly good physical condition. 'You're as young as you feel' isn't just a truism: there is scientific evidence that a person's inner attitude has a significant influence on his or her vitality and activity.

Many of the menopausal symptoms described above cannot merely be explained by the hormone change. The psychological symptoms especially can be traced back to a fostered fear of the menopause. Beside

Once their children have moved out, many mothers have the feeling of no longer being needed. Don't take on new (e.g. voluntary) responsibilities rashly. Think about postponed desires and dreams that you could now fulfil. For example, when was the last time you had a room to yourself? How about making you child's now empty room your own?

Self-help groups are available for women who are at the beginning or already in the midst of their menopause. Here, you can not only find understanding 'fellow sufferers', but also have the chance of making new acquaintances and friends, e.g. after an extended family break.

your general condition, your family situation, background, surroundings and inner attitude to menopause play an important role in experiencing and coping with this phase of your life.

Having to reassign familiar tasks within the family can bring about a serious crisis in a lot of women. When the children have moved out from home, a lot of mothers tend to fall into despair. The sudden feeling of no longer being needed can lead to depression. Similarly, returning to living purely in a partnership after leading an existence as a parent for a long time is a fundamental change which can frequently cause problems.

Some women experience menopause as a serious identity crisis. They fear menopause as being the time when they finally have to bid farewell to their youth once and for all and are afraid of losing their sex appeal along with their fertility. They are also afraid of no longer being attractive and of having to lose esteem, affection and prestige with advancing age.

However, there is no real need for this last-minute panic: sexual pleasure is not linked to fertility. And if you look around to your acquaintances, you will realise that a lot of very attractive women do not correspond to the classic ideal of beauty, but that their charisma is closely linked to their individuality, their happiness, their warm-heartedness or their sense of humour.

To some extent, it is in your own hands how you experience and cope with the menopause. If you accept the fact that a new phase in your life is beginning and that you are aging, you will often only suffer minimally from the physical and psychological symptoms of the climacteric.

Now is the time to use your wealth of life experience primarily for your own good. Take stock: what do you want? What to you need to feel good? Especially for mothers, it is a significant change to suddenly start thinking more about themselves and to set about reorganising their lives.

You can't change your biological age, but you can certainly influence your mental age: if you go through life with alert senses and open eyes, you will find that not only does your life seem longer, but your years have been filled with life. Don't merely bow to the constraints of traditional standards and values. Who says you're too old to try out something new? What's keeping you from joining a tango course in your mid-fifties, or starting to scuba dive if you are in good physical condition? By opening new horizons, you can lay the foundation for a fulfilled old age right now.

Be good to yourself! Make sure you get sufficient exercise, but also treat yourself to some relaxing hours. Keep up your hobbies and other interests. Stay in touch with your friends and maintain your social acquaintances. Social contacts characterised by mutual goodwill are active health care: attention and affection not only make you feel happy, they are also good for your health.

Your relationship also plays an important role in this connection: a regular dose of tender loving care will balance your personality, help you to cope with stress and even stimulate your immune system. Make plans together,

Especially with sleeping disorders, a lot of women are quick to take tablets, barbiturates or tranquillisers. Such highly effective drugs should only be taken on the advice of your doctor and in the recommended dosage. If he prescribes psychiatric drugs to be taken for longer than a week, you should ask him to explain the reasons to you in detail. An excessively carefree handling of these drugs can quickly lead to addiction. Frequently, herbal remedies are very efficient in treating mood shifts or sleeping disorders.

do things together, share interests and take time to talk – that's how your relationship will become more intense and resilient.

Try to adopt a positive attitude to things in general – follow the motto that optimists not only have a longer but also a happier life. Don't avoid problems: look for constructive solutions. Women who take their life into their own hands are less at risk of suffering from depression.

Even if you are feeling sad or melancholic, don't let others pressure you, and don't pressure yourself. Suggestions such as "Pull yourself together!" or "Why don't you go on a holiday – that will take your mind off things" are not very helpful. Accept the fact that you just don't feel like laughing at the moment.

If your spirits are low frequently, herbal remedies such as St. John's wort or kava-kava can be useful. However, if you can't make it through the psychological crisis on your own, you might be suffering from serious depression. In this case you should urgently seek professional assistance.

Acute menopausal complaints can be quite an ordeal. Don't try to be a hero: if you find you are constantly suffering from serious restrictions, the benefits of a temporary hormone treatment will outweigh the drawbacks. Carefully selecting the drug, balancing it precisely to your needs and regular check-ups can further reduce your risks.

HORMONE TREATMENT – THE CASE FOR AND AGAINST

If you are really suffering during menopause, you should consult your physician. Nowadays, a variety of medical remedies are available, which can make the unpleasant symptoms more tolerable. One possibility is hor-

mone replacement therapy, where your body is supplied with the missing hormones for a certain period of time.

Even today, the benefits and drawbacks of hormone treatment to relieve physical and psychological symptoms of menopause are still disputed. On the one hand, patients are intimidated again and again by horror stories according to which hormone therapy encourages the development of cancer. On the other hand, some doctors sell such a treatment as a true miracle cure that is not only able to provide relief from menopausal symptoms but can protect you against all kinds of other diseases, too.

The findings from research into a supposedly higher risk of cancer of the uterus and breast cancer in connection with hormone treatment are somewhat contradictory. Whereas some scientists see a connection here, others are convinced of the opposite, i.e. that hormone replacement therapy in fact reduces the risk of cancer. That's why the outcome of an extremely extensive long-range study currently involving about 27,000 women in the U.S. is eagerly awaited. The 'Woman's Health Initiative' is being sponsored by American health organisations, but no results can be expected until 2005.

However, you shouldn't put up with serious symptoms of the menopause for years on end merely out of fear of the risks of hormone replacement therapy. It is quite sensible to treat some of the symptoms with hormones, especially if this treatment is only short-term. It is primarily long-term treatment (longer than 5 years) that is suspected of increasing the risk of cancer. In the case of many symptoms, a treatment of two to five years is sufficient.

Hormone replacement therapy or hormone substitution is a temporary supply of hormones that are no longer or no longer sufficiently produced by your own body. In general, the goal of such a treatment is to alleviate the unpleasant symptoms of the hormone deficiency.

Even if you decide to undergo hormone treatment, don't expect a miracle: hormones are neither a cure-all nor a fountain of youth. To remain physically fit to an advanced age, it is not enough to simply take medication; you must take the initiative to adopt an active life-style – with healthy nourishment, adequate physical exercise and by avoiding toxins such as alcohol and nicotine.

To prevent cardiovascular diseases, a long-term treatment of more than five years is considered necessary, and as much as eight to ten years are required to prevent osteoporosis. The longer you are to take the hormones, the more carefully the advantages and risks must be weighed up against each other. Apart from the intensity of your complaints, your individual health risks – which a doctor will determine in the course of a thorough examination – play an important role in deciding whether hormone treatment is suitable for you or not.

If your doctor considers hormone substitution advisable in view of your problems, you should make sure he explains the type and length of the intended treatment. Your doctor should take care to inform you about the expected benefits and the possible drawbacks. If you are then still uncertain about hormone treatment, you shouldn't hesitate to get a second opinion.

In general, the main reason for treating menopause symptoms with hormones is to supply the body with oestrogen in order to balance out the symptoms of an oestrogen deficiency. Women who have had a hysterectomy can be treated with pure oestrogen. Those who still have their womb, however, shouldn't take pure oestrogen as it stimulates the growth of the endometrium. And if this is constantly stimulated without being shed, growths may result; the risk of cells becoming malignant increases.

Before you decide for or against hormone replacement therapy, your doctor should examine you thoroughly to eliminate possible risks. The following steps are part of the examination:
- an examination of the breasts and abdomen
- a smear test to detect cancer of the cervix
- possibly a mammography
- measurement of your blood pressure
- stool analysis (to eliminate cancer of the intestine or stomach)
- a check of liver and gall bladder function
- investigating your own and your family's medical history to find possible risks. These can be diabetes, epilepsy, smoking, high blood pressure, susceptibility to thrombosis, myoma and other disorders of the womb, gall problems, migraine, sickle cell anaemia as well as a family history of breast cancer.

A variety of treatments that supply the body with oestrogen as well as progesterone are available for these patients.

There are two kinds of hormone therapy: phase and combination therapy. In phase therapy, the intake emulates a menstrual cycle of 22 or 28 days; you start by taking oestrogen and then, halfway through the process, you will be given a combination of oestrogen and gestagen. With some treatments, the intake has to be interrupted for a few days each month. Slight bleeding tends to occur at this time, although it stops eventually. In combination therapy, oestrogen and gestagen are taken simultaneously and without interruption. With this kind of treatment, periods usually stop quite soon.

The decision as to whether to go along with hormone therapy and the choice of treatment also depends on what stage of menopause you are in and what kind of symptoms you suffer from. If your period stops before you turn 40, hormone replacement theory is generally recommended. This kind of treatment can also provide considerable relief against very strong hot flushes and sweats occurring before menopause.

Hormone therapy can also be appropriate if your family background or other risk factors suggest an increased susceptibility to osteoporosis. The intake of oestrogen can significantly slow down the decrease of bone mass, thereby lowering the risk of bone fracture. Ideally, such an oestrogen therapy is combined with supporting measures such as a diet rich in protein and calcium, regular physical activity and – in already existing serious cases of osteoporosis – the intake of fluorides.

After menopause, the risk of cardiovascular diseases is increased. Previously, the body's own oestrogen functioned as a natural shield against the calcification of arteries and provided some protection against heart attacks and strokes. Whether a hormone treatment to reduce these risks is recommendable is the topic of controversial discussion. The predominant medical opinion seems to be that in this case, the benefits outweigh the drawbacks.

You shouldn't, however, expect miracles from hormone replacement therapy: not all of your complaints will disappear if you take hormones. Hormones are no fountain of youth, and hormone replacement therapy cannot reduce your wrinkles or stop you from aging.

In reality, hormone therapy means interfering with your body's natural processes, and that's why it should be given careful consideration. Possible
side-effects of such a treatment are, for example, nausea (especially in
the first three months), headaches, weight gain, oedema and painful
swelling of the chest. Some women also complain of dry, blemished skin or
skin rashes. Cramps in the calves and problems with the gall bladder may
occur in connection with hormone substitution, as well as metabolism
disorders, increased discharge and a higher blood pressure. Occasionally,
hormone treatment can lead to loss of hair, itching and secretions from
the nipples. An overdose is frequently the cause of such side-effects; the
hormone level should then be reduced accordingly. You should consult
your doctor if you notice any unusual changes, especially heavy bleeding,
during the treatment.

The amount of oestrogen that has to be supplied to the body can vary
from one woman to the next. Some women already notice a definite improvement of their condition with low hormone doses, while others need a
higher dose. This also depends on how much oestrogen your body is still
producing itself.

Apart from oral treatment, your doctor can also give you an injection
every six to eight weeks that ensures a gradual, controlled release of
hormones. Hormone plasters that continuously supply the active substances to your body need to be changed twice a week, and a one-week
break is recommended after every three weeks of treatment. Local treatment is also possible, for example extreme vaginal dryness can be treated
with creams or suppositories containing oestrogen. It is also advisable to
interrupt this treatment every now and then.

DHEA AND MELATONIN –
RISK-FREE ANTI-AGING HORMONES?

Melatonin is a hormone produced by the hypothalamus. This substance,
which is provided in larger quantities when there is no daylight, gives the
pulse to our inner body clock. Abroad, melatonin has been available
as a food supplement for years, just as vitamins and trace elements are.
In Germany, it was briefly available as such even though it was not licensed.

Nor is it licensed as a medication, because proof of its benefits and harm-lessness are yet to be published. However, it can be sold as 'imported medication' in German pharmacies. Though melatonin has been pre-sented by the media as life-prolonging substance and a 'miracle drug' against Alzheimer's, sleeping disorders, AIDS and cancer, it may have side-effects. It is for example suspected of causing eye problems. Because melatonin has a lasting effect on the body's own regulation processes, it should only be taken with medical advice and under medical observation.

The same is true of another so-called 'anti-aging hormone': DHEA (dehydroepiandrosterone), a steroid hormone which the adrenal glands produce from cholesterol. The body produces only a small amount of DHEA in infancy; the level then increases from the age of six or seven and reaches its climax when we are about 25 years old. From the age of 30 onwards, the production continuously decreases until – by the age of 75 – its concentration in the blood amounts to only about 20% of that of a 25-year-old. This leads to the conclusion that DHEA deficiency is respon-sible for signs of old age.

This is the reason why – in the U.S. – DHEA is promoted as a drug that slows down the aging process. It is not only supposed to provide the body with renewed energy, lift your spirits and get the immune system going, but is also said to help against high blood pressure, obesity and lack of sexual desire. Reliable medical insights into the effectiveness of artificially sup-plied DHEA are almost non-existent. An improvement in well-being has only been observed in women with long-term adrenal gland insufficiency.

DHEA is not licensed for the German market, but it can be sold in the U.S. as a food supplement. Because sufficient research into possible side-effects is still lacking, you should certainly consult your doctor before experiment-ing with such a hormone treatment yourself.

NATURAL REMEDIES FOR MENOPAUSAL COMPLAINTS

An addition to hormone replacement therapy, quite a number of natural remedies exist with which you can relieve menopausal complaints. For example, some natural cures such as acupuncture or homeopathy can occasionally help.

It also makes sense to critically analyse your habits. These have an influence on your susceptibility to cardiovascular problems or osteoporosis, for instance, that should not be underestimated. For example, women who are very overweight often suffer more from menopausal complaints and are more susceptible to illness; therefore, a balanced , low-fat diet is very sensible.

You can stimulate your metabolism by means of alternating hot and cold showers, regular swimming or daily gymnastics. Brisk walks are also very good: daylight and the sun's radiation really get your metabolism going. In addition, you should smoke as little as possible and drink hardly any alcohol. These luxury goods have negative effects on your metabolism, increase the risk of cardiovascular illnesses and – just like abundant coffee consumption – susceptibility to osteoporosis.

A good deal of outdoor exercise not only strengthens your bones and thus helps prevent osteoporosis – if you exercise regularly, you will stay healthy and flexible and feel more at home in your own body.

Apart from leading a healthier life, there are also a variety of herbal remedies that you can use for specific complaints. Fluctuation in mood, for example, can be treated with Bach flower remedy in some women.

When using herbal remedies, you should observe a few important points:

- Even herbal remedies are highly effective substances, which you should not take carelessly. If you are taking any for a prolonged period of time, you should consult your doctor.

- Don't take several herbal remedies at the same time. This will help you avoid undesired interactive effects.

- Medication containing substances that are similar to oestrogen should only be taken in consultation with your doctor and only if you are still having periods. These substances can lead to growths on the endometrium.

- Especially with medicinal plants, it can take a while for them to have the desired effect. Be patient and don't go from one remedy to the next – this, too, can protect you against unwanted interaction.

The following are the most important medicinal plants:

- If you suffer from hot flushes, two cups of sage tea daily can help you. Sage not only has an anti inflammatory effect but also inhibits sweating. You should not, however, continue a sage tea cure indefinitely. Shepherd's-purse can also provide relief from hot flushes.

- Fructus agnus castus is a verbena officinalis plant that is widely used in gynaecology. It has similar effects to the corpus luteum. Preparations with this plant are used primarily against period pains and problems occurring at the beginning of menopause. Also, this medicinal plant is said to have a positive effect on the vegetative nervous system. Rosemary can also be used to treat period disorders. This traditional medicinal plant is also very useful for nervous agitation.

- Cimicifuga racemosa has a similar effect to oestrogen on the regulating mechanism of the menstrual cycle and influences the ovaries and uterus.

You should treat your spine with special care from the menopause onwards at the very latest. Rather than carrying heavy shopping bags, you should use a shopper. Heavy objects should be lifted from a crouching position – then your legs will bear part of the strain. At night, a firm mattress will give your back the support it needs.

Especially if you have problems in holding back urine, you should make sure you drink enough – at least 3 pints over the course of the day. If you drink too little, you will be more prone to urinary tract infections, and frequent infections can increase incontinence.

It alleviates typical menopausal problems such as hot flushes, sweating, palpitations, restlessness, agitation, irritability, dizziness and headaches and is also said to help with depression. Unfortunately, it is ineffective against osteoporosis.

- If you are suffering from incontinence, substances containing aletris farinosa can enhance the success of pelvic floor exercises. Preparations containing this plant are said to strengthen the pelvic floor muscles. Infections of the kidneys or urethra can be treated with horsetail. This substance will also give added gloss to your hair and strengthen your fingernails. Melilotus altissima preparations have a diuretic effect and are good with urinary tract infections. They are also useful in treating water retention, cramps in the calves and sleeping disorders.

- Restlessness and irritability, often combined with sleeping disorders, frequently accompany menopause. Nature has a number of remedies at hand to help reduce tension and lift your spirits. Taken regularly as drops, tablets or tea, St. John's wort has a relaxing and calming effect and improves your sleep. The kava-kava bush can be found in the South Pacific. Kava-kava preparations relieve tension and anxiety and promote sleep. Hop is also useful for nervous exhaustion and sleeping disorders, has anti-inflammatory effects (especially for your bladder and skin), and calms your intestines. One of the bitter substances contained in hop is similar to oestrogen in its effects on the body.

- Whitethorn tea can be effective in treating anxiety, palpitations and sleeping disorders. Valerian is also a useful natural tranquilliser. It is available as tea or in tablet form and helps you to feel relaxed, balanced and less irritable and will help you sleep. Fluctuations in mood and exhaustion can also be treated with balm tea. This aromatic herb acts as a muscle relaxant and will help you to sleep better.

- Lady's coat is widely used in homoeopathy. It relieves tension and stimulates the metabolism. Preparations can be very effective in treating urinary tract disorders. This medicinal plant helps treat a variety of menopausal problems such as hot flushes and sweating, depression, listlessness and irritability. The classic menopausal complaints can also be treated with lycopus europeaus.

HOW TO PROTECT YOURSELF AGAINST OSTEOPOROSIS

Preventive measures are the be-all and end-all when it comes to dealing with osteoporosis. The sooner you start actively doing something, the better. A healthy life-style before the menopause will reduce your risk of suffering from this reduction in bone mass.

Continue to ensure that you eat enough fruit, vegetables and dairy products. You should be taking at least 1000 milligrams of calcium, and sufficient vitamin D. This can't completely stop the loss of bone mass, but can slow it down. Avoid alcohol and nicotine. These substances, as well as coffee, increase your susceptibility to osteoporosis.

If you think you could have an inherited susceptibility to osteoporosis, a hormone treatment could be advisable. This will significantly lower the risk of fractures. Even if the process of bone reduction has already begun, it can be slowed down or even stopped with hormone treatment, because oestrogen supports the skeleton's absorption of calcium. However, you should be aware of the fact that bone reduction will begin again as soon as you stop taking the hormones. This is why a hormone treatment of osteoporosis can take several years.

A calcitonin treatment can be a possible alternative to the prophylactic intake of oestrogen. This hormone also supports calcium absorption by the bones, and certain amounts of it are produced by your thyroid gland.

When used as a therapeutic substance, it is injected and the patient also has to ensure a high calcium intake. However, such treatment cannot prevent fractures in an already existing case of osteoporosis. Serious osteoporosis is additionally treated with fluorides; however, these are ineffective for one patient in three.

If you are suffering from osteoporosis, then you should keep a close eye on the progress of this disorder. This is mostly done by means of the bone mass index, which is determined by a bone density measurement and an X-ray, normally of the wrist.

PELVIC FLOOR WEAKNESS AND PELVIC FLOOR EXERCISES

One of the most frequent and unpleasant problems encountered during and after menopause is urinary incontinence. Uncontrolled loss of urine frequently occurs as a result of sudden convulsions – laughing, sneezing, coughing, but also running – and when lifting heavy objects. There are various reasons for this. One is that your bladder and urethra shrink due to the lack of oestrogen. The tissue becomes thinner and more sensitive to stimulation. In severe cases, the bladder sphincter slackens to such an extent that urine can no longer be held back. Another reason is that the muscles and ligaments supporting the bladder and urethra slacken with progressing age. However, diabetes or urinary tract infections are also possible causes incontinence. This is why the cause should definitely be determined in a medical examination.

If there is no underlying illness, the problem can be solved by performing specific exercises. Perhaps you are already familiar with the exercises that strengthen the pelvic floor from prenatal classes? These can strengthen the muscles that support the bladder and urethra. When you urinate, sit on the toilet with your legs apart and try to interrupt the flow of urine several times. The muscles you use to do this are the ones we are talking about. Get into the habit of doing this exercise whenever you go to the toilet. Once you have developed a feeling for the sphincters around the urethra, vagina and anus, you should attempt to deliberately tense them and hold the tension for a while. You should count to five at first, and later you can hold the

Certain exercises can help you to train and strengthen the pelvic floor muscles. A complex fitness plan isn't necessary – you can do these inconspicuous exercises anywhere, at any time.

tension for a longer period of time. That can be while you're waiting for the traffic lights to turn green, in the lift, or during a commercial break on TV. You should continue breathing calmly and regularly. Then, consciously relax the muscles and imagine how your abdomen opens up as you release the tension; repeat this a few times. Ideally, you should perform this exercise several times a day.

THE MALE MENOPAUSE – A CHANGE OF LIFE FOR MEN TOO

Recently, the phenomenon of the 'male menopause' has been the subject of much discussion. For quite some years, these male symptoms of aging were either elegantly paraphrased as the 'mid-life crisis' or modestly kept secret.

This is why the realisation that men suffer from some of the same symptoms is a rather recent one. These symptoms include loss of sexual desire, impotence, hot flushes and sweating, buzzing in the ears, dizziness and palpitations, along with sleeping disorders, fluctuations in mood, aggression and even outbursts of rage, weaker urine flow, increased cholesterol levels, weight gain, and also disturbances of memory and concentration or aches and pains in the muscles and joints.

To use 'male menopause' in this context wouldn't be quite appropriate though, because the male hormone level does not sink nearly as rapidly as that of women: it sinks gradually over a longer period of time. The symptoms described above can occur in men between 30 and 90 years of age, whereas the female menopause is limited to the time between 45 and 55 years.

Doctors sometimes recommend a hormone therapy to treat the menopausal complaints in men. In this case, the male hormone testosterone is used. But in men, too, this treatment is quite controversial. Viagra can sometimes help with potency problems. Natural remedies, however, can also help to avoid or reduce many of the unpleasant symptoms. Changing to a balanced diet comprising a lot of fruit and vegetables and only a little meat can be advisable. Men should also drink a lot – up to five or six pints per day. Fresh carrot, celery and apple juice can be very helpful. Your partner should drink at least a pint of this mixture per day, slowly and in small sips. Alcoholic beverages should be avoided, and if possible he shouldn't smoke. Regular exercise can not only prevent weight gain and possible depression, but also trains your partner's muscles and stimulates the effectiveness of the remaining male hormones.

Think about what your partner needs now – someone who will listen to him, some physical contact, or simply some peace and quiet?

RELATIONSHIP AND LOVE-LIFE

The image that a lot of women (and men) have of the menopause is characterised by superficial knowledge and preconceptions. A lot of what we think we know about menopause is nothing but a myth. During this phase of a woman's life, she neither turns into a hysterical bundle of nerves with uncontrollable emotional outbursts, nor does she automatically lose her ability to have a fulfilled sex life because of sinking hormone levels. Menopause is often a time of change for a relationship, but the woman's physical condition is not the only cause of this. Men must also make their contribution towards giving the relationship a firm foundation for the years to come.

YOU AND ME – REDISCOVERING YOUR PARTNER

The menopause takes place between about your mid-forties and late fifties. Apart from the physical changes described in chapter two, a lot of other things happen during this time that have far-reaching effects on your daily life and your future.

In terms of professional life, for example, the agenda has long since been set – unless you are trying to return to a job after taking a family break. If you have children, they can now cater for themselves. If you have involuntarily had no children, the time of hope and anxiety is now gradually coming to an end. Now at the very latest, you should start designing a plan for your life that will fulfil you and make you happy – even without having a child.

If you are living in a long-term relationship, this will be faced with new challenges, because parallel to the circumstances of life, relationships are exposed to constant change. Some couples discover their togetherness anew once the children have moved out from home and in this context discover new or long-forgotten feelings for each other. In other couples, your partner becomes interesting again once his job and career are no longer at the centre of his life.

In a worst-case scenario, couples have to finally admit just how far they have drifted apart. Since the children or the job can no longer provide distraction, conflicts that have been suppressed for a long time will now come to the surface. During this time, quite a number of couples are faced with some questions: Do we still love each other? Do we still like each other? Or have we only stayed together for the sake of the children? Are we perhaps only going through the motions in our marriage out of habit or for fear of change?

Frequently, a lot of things that happened in the past are taking full effect now: disappointed expectations, unfulfilled hopes, deliberate and accidental insults and hurts.

Quite a few marriages break up during this time. Some people venture into a new beginning with a new partner, others – voluntarily or involuntarily –

stay alone. And in a lot of lasting relationships, the balance shifts: whereas up to now, it was the man who had the say, with progressing age – and especially after the man has retired – it is often the woman who gradually takes over. This new form of living together must also be carefully balanced out.

Both you and your partner are now confronted with the thought of aging, you often find it difficult to adjust to this. It is just as difficult for men as for women to accept the inner and outer changes. But only if you both accept and admit these changes can you regard this phase as an active chance for a new beginning. The most important prerequisite for this is being open, fair and honest with each other.

Talking with Each Other – Nothing Could be Simpler

Over the course of time, a lot of couples forget how to talk with each other. Of course you talk in order to co-ordinate day-to-day life. But if you ask them when they last had a long, detailed chat about something essential – for example, about shared interests or something that is on one of their minds – a lot of couples cannot give you an answer.

That's why you should try to rediscover each other over and over again. Can you still remember what that person you fell in love with back then was like? He's still there – he's merely aged. Think about how you could take up the old times: What did you use to do together? What did you both enjoy? What could you laugh about together and what did you have heated discussions about even then?

In fact, however, the first person you have to rediscover is yourself. What can you enthuse about? What do you particularly like doing? Where are your personal strengths? The answers to these questions will guide you; try to allow time for these needs. Look for people who compement you in this respect. Shared interests are a good foundation for friendship and more…

Communication is vital for a relationship. Don't evade your partner if he wants to talk with you. If you're not in the mood for an intensive discussion, don't turn your partner away with lame excuses. If you feel too tired, too busy, too irritable or too angry for a discussion, just say so!

With progressing age, the probability of living alone, either voluntarily or involuntarily, increases for women. Old age is a typically female phenomenon: already in the mid-eighties, more than two thirds of the above 60s were women, of whom more than half were living on their own.

On the other hand, you shouldn't let yourself be forced into a discussion that you don't feel up to at this moment in time. In such a case, it is better to suggest an alternative date and then stick to it. That's how you can show your partner that you take his desire to talk seriously. Neither should you force him into a discussion that he doesn't want to have just at the moment. But do ask when it would be convenient to discuss the issues at hand, and then bring up the matter again at a suitable time.

Find out in which situations you can talk especially well and undisturbed. Some couples find long car trips a good opportunity, for others it is walks they take together. With tricky topics, it makes sense to keep your hands occupied (e.g. with gardening or the dishes). This can serve as an outlet for the tension connected with the topic.

It would be an illusion and also far too exhausting to want to share every thought and emotion with your partner, although couples who have a

ARGUING IS A MATTER OF PRACTICE

Especially with controversial topics, it can be difficult to stay calm and fair. Any argument can easily turn into a power struggle. There is great potential for conflict if the argument merely serves as an excuse for conducting a battle about fundamental problems.

In addition to this, a couple that has already lived together for quite a long time will more easily fall into their arguing routine and start pointlessly accusing and blaming each other instead of constructively talking matters through.

Try to find a common basis for discussion and define a few simple rules for arguing to which you will both adhere. That's how you can develop an arguing technique and will more easily be able to avoid your relationship traps. Here are a few suggestions:

- We like each other. We're not facing each other as enemies; we just have different opinions.
- It's not a matter of being right out of principle. There is no winner at the other's expense. We want to find a solution we can both live with.
- We will not interrupt each other and will treat one another with respect.
- We will concentrate on the issue at hand, and not attempt a sweeping blow. Earlier 'transgressions' have nothing to do with this discussion.
- If one of us wants to end the discussion, they can simply say that. We will try to find an acceptable solution at a later time.

clear understanding of each other's desires, dreams, and problems tend to be much more understanding and sensitive with each other. They can adapt to each other much easier and experience their relationship as being harmonious and happy.

Of course, it isn't always easy to understand each other and to feel with your partner in every situation and phase of his life. That's why it is all the more important to talk about what is bothering you. Especially during menopause, this can be a relief to both partners. If your partner isn't completely surprised by your mood shifts, he won't feel treated unfairly if you do lose it. If he knows you are afraid of no longer being attractive, he might attempt to cut back on some humorously intended remarks that you could perceive as hurtful in your current situation.

Let your partner know whenever he can do something useful for you. For example, if you feel a hot flush coming on at a party, ask him to go outside with you or to bring you a glass of water. He won't be able to anticipate your every wish, of course, but he will often be relieved if he can help you somehow or other.

If you are longing for more attention, support, understanding and affection, it is certainly sensible to let your partner have some of this too. On the other hand, that alone won't be sufficient. Whether you want him to help you around the house or just massage your aching back: ask him, don't wait for him to notice himself. You will avoid disappointment and make life a lot easier for both of you.

Couples who are sensitive to each other's needs, and who manage to re-kindle interest in one another again and again, often have a very intense relationship. This not only gives them emotional certainty and strength, but is also essential to a satisfying sexual relationship.

DON'T FEAR A LOSS OF SEXUAL DESIRE

A lot of women fear menopause because as far as they're concerned, it is then at the latest that the matter of sex is closed for them. There are often a variety of reasons for this. For example, some women still think that the hormones produced in their ovaries regulate their sexual desire. But

It is a fallacy to think that your partner can work out what you want with a little bit of good will (or if he really loves you). If you expect things to happen along these lines, then you are building traps that your partner simply has to fall into. Let's be honest: more often than not, our most intimate dreams and desires are well hidden secrets. Surely, a sensitive and attentive partner will be able to guess a few of them. But why don't you try to make life a little easier for both of you?

If you feel good about yourself before menopause and manage to keep this self-confidence, you'll be able to enjoy your sexuality well into old age and be much more carefree and less inhibited.

there is no connection – sexual experience is not related to the ability to get pregnant.

Research has shown that sexual desire in women remains fairly constant between their mid-thirties and far beyond the end of menopause. According to other studies, women experience their sexuality as being more intense and more pleasurable around the age of forty. Whereas men tend to be more sexually active in their younger years, women frequently only reach the height of their sexual experience in mid-life. And apparently, this doesn't change a lot until they reach an advanced age.

The oestrogen produced in the ovaries therefore can't be solely responsible for women's sexual desire. Androgenes, the male hormones produced in a woman's body, apparently play an important role in this respect. These hormones are produced in the adrenal glands, which is why their production is not affected by menopause. On the contrary, their influence increases – which is another reason why some women even enjoy sex more after their menopause.

However, oestrogen plays a significant role in keeping the vagina lubricated and flexible. If the level of oestrogen sinks, the mucous membranes change. In some women, vaginal dryness – even with strong sexual arousal – causes pain during intercourse. In this case you should consult your doctor. In some women it merely takes longer for the vagina to become lubricated and to stretch. Here, longer and more intensive foreplay is needed to be able to enjoy making love.

In this regard, too, you have to keep in practice. An active sex-life contributes to the proper functioning of your sexual organs. So, if you have a partner with whom you can completely enjoy sex, do so by all means. Just because your body is aging doesn't mean that your love for each other has to do so too.

If your love-life has become somewhat dreary with the years, then you and your partner should think about whether you want to change this. A fulfilled love-life not only keeps you physically fit (for example, sexually active women suffer much less from menopausal problems) and strengthens your confidence, but also strengthens and enhances your relationship.

PROFESSIONAL HELP FOR SERIOUS PROBLEMS

Human sexuality is a complex interaction of physical, psychological, social and environmental aspects. For example, emotional stress can seriously inhibit your sexual desire.

This could be the case if
- you have drifted apart to such an extent that you have lost trust in and desire for each other.

- on the contrary, you have become so familiar with each other that there is no longer any curiosity or sexual tension between you.

- one or both of you are having difficulties in admitting your sexual desires or is denying them out of embarrassment.

- problems from other areas of your life are constantly on the mind of one of you or is troubling you.

- one of you is suffering from a serious illness and you haven't yet found a way of dealing with this together.

Physical problems can also significantly affect your love-life. Age-related problems in intercourse can already occur in your mid-thirties. Apart from biological impotence in men, these can also be caused by a constant

hormone deficiency in women. The physical changes during and after menopause mostly affect the organs oestrogen is needed for: your uterus, vagina, vulva and mammary glands. These might regress due to the changed hormone levels and the reduced circulation. Your tissues might shrink and become more susceptible to infection, which could be accompanied by inflammatory changes.

Since the natural balance of bacteria in the vagina is also affected by menopause, a lot of women suffer from painful vaginal itching. In some women, the vaginal lining secretes less and less mucus with progressing age. This can result in problems during intercourse. Understandably, all these physical restrictions can significantly interfere with your sexual desires.

Talk to your gynaecologist about this. There are a number of remedies to provide relief for problems related to intercourse. A lot of these treatments are very simple and straightforward. Vaginal dryness, for example, can possibly be treated with creams containing oestrogen.

A woman's hormone balance significantly changes during menopause. For a long time, people assumed that the reduced hormone production was responsible for the increased loss of sexual desire perceived by some women. But certainly not all difficulties occurring during menopause are a result of the changing hormone levels or make a hormone treatment absolutely necessary.

Loss of sexual desire is frequently due to emotional imbalance. As research has shown, in this case, preparations containing St. John's wort can have

Befriend your body – it's been a good companion to you for decades. Why shouldn't it be allowed to age and mature together with you? Why on earth should a woman of fifty have the body of a young girl?

a very positive effect on the female sexuality during the climacterium. St. John's wort extracts improve the function of your nerves and lift your spirits – with no side-effects.

If you notice serious problems with sexuality in yourself or your partner which you cannot solve on your own, it is sensible to seek professional help. You certainly shouldn't just give up and consider the topic of sexuality closed, but enlist the help of a professional. However, the causes of undue inactivity in bed are rarely so dramatic that a couple can't resolve them together.

Of course, some women gratefully take their menopause as an excuse to end a dissatisfying sexual relationship. But far more frequently, it is health problems in the husband that are responsible for the end of conjugal sexuality. Many women have a sexual desire until far beyond their menopause. Often the biggest problem is the lack of a suitable partner. With progressing age, the percentage of women who do not live in a long-term relationship increases. They are either widowed or divorced and find looking for a new partner more difficult than men at the same age, for whom it is still easier to find a partner who is often younger.

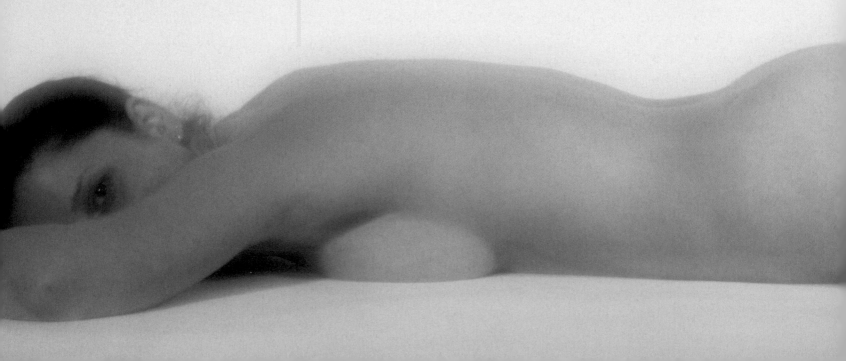

AM I GOOD-LOOKING?
ABOUT AGING

The sex-life of some women suffers from their fear of not being attractive enough – and often for a life-time. Unfortunately, it is indeed the case that still very different standards apply to men and women when it comes to people perceiving them as being attractive or not. And this is even more so with increasing age. "Women get old and men more interesting" – this s a popular phrase. For women, the beauty ideal of having to be 'young, slim and possibly without wrinkles' is still valid to a much stronger degree. Recently, however, men have been confronted with more demanding standards, as is reflected by the rising number of male clients and patients of beauticians and cosmetic surgeons.

It is obvious, however, that you can only keep up with our society's mania for youth for a limited period of time. Therefore, having a healthy dose of self-confidence that is not exclusively based on your physical appearance is not only important for women. If you are at peace and in harmony with yourself, it will be much easier for you to accept that your body shows signs of age. Of course it does – after all, you've been living your life!

There's no point in mourning the body of your youth. Back then you were a different person to who you are today – on the inside as well as the outside. Would you honestly want to slip back into the (admittedly immaculate) body of the insecure teenager you once were?

Stand in front of the mirror every now and then and recite your bonuses out aloud. Try not to be at odds with those parts of your body that you dislike, but rather focus on those you are pleased with. Cultivate and uphold this positive image of yourself. Don't mourn that which you may have lost in looks, but stand by what you have become as a person. If you are satisfied and at peace with yourself, you will have charisma and will be attractive, even if your body isn't immaculate and doesn't (any longer) conform to the current ideal of beauty.

Accept your body just as it is. Don't try to force it into being as it used to be. Of course, that doesn't mean that you should let yourself go. On the contrary: look after your body, care for it – but do it for yourself and your

Especially when you are getting older, the relationship to a partner your age is a lot easier in many aspects. You have both already learned to lead your own lives, have developed a mature personality and are more capable of respecting the other's personality without wanting to change it to match your own ideas.

own well-being, and not to satisfy other people's real or supposed notions of the ideal. Frequently, they will size you up much less harshly than you do yourself.

Recently, more and more men have come to realise that such qualities as experience and maturity, self-confidence, charm, serenity and tolerance are positive and desirable features in a woman that are worth more than youthful looks. Quite a number of actresses could spring to mind here. Even power women such as Tina Turner or Sophia Loren impress a lot of people with their confidence and charisma, without making a secret of their age or their wrinkles.

TREADING NEW PATHS – TIME FOR AFFECTION

The desire for being touched, for affection and physical contact is a basic need with which humans are endowed at birth. In the course of our lives, we develop a variety of means of expressing our emotions. Our sexuality is one of these means of expression. If you deny or suppress it, you block off an important part of your emotional life.

The widespread assumption that interest in sex is automatically lost with progressing age is completely erroneous. Even beyond menopause, people are generally speaking by no means asexual beings, but have distinct sexual needs and are quite active in bed. However, sexuality is subject to changes over the course of a person's life. Your bodily functions gradually wind down and your stamina can also wane. Yet, that doesn't have to affect your passion, if you adjust to each other lovingly and emphatically.

In practically every relationship, phases of intense passion alternate with longer breaks. That in itself is no reason for concern. However, if your sexual slackness lasts for an excessive amount of time, you should try to find out the reasons for this. Often, the main cause of the change is not due to physical problems, but to a lack of confidence, pressure or wrong expectations.

For example, the (older) partner is often the reason why women have less sex after menopause than younger women. This lies in the fact that the nat-

Many parts of the human body give rise to a feeling of sexual desire when caressed. Erogenous zones can not only be found around your genitals. Your back, neck, and ears can also react very sensitively to tender affection. Mutually discovering such areas on your body and incorporating them into your love-life can be a passionate and enhancing experience.

ural side-effects of aging affect the 'strong sex' much more than women. It can take him longer to get an erection; and at an advanced age the erection can often not be maintained for very long.

For fear of 'failing' at the crucial moment and embarrassing themselves in front of their partner, many (not only older) men would rather completely avoid sexual intercourse. For it is primarily men who are affected by pressure of performing well even in bed. A lot of men consider a spontaneous, strong erection as their right by nature. If they fail to have an erection, they feel cheated by their body and are deeply affected in their male confidence.

A lot of men are simply not aware that a lot of things just go more slowly with increasing age and that this also affects their bodily functions. So they put themselves under additional pressure by unnecessarily fearing failure – and a result they often can't perform at all. Instead of attempting to 'repair' this supposed 'defect' with Viagra or some such remedy, it would often suffice if they were more understanding with their own body. The experience and feelings that partners have with each other are particularly important. Quite frequently, men regain their sexuality if they manage to be sexually active without focussing on having an erection.

In our society, sexual attraction is still often equated with having a slim, youthful body. In the erroneous assumption that their own waning physical attraction is the cause for loss of sexual desire in their partner, a lot of women still accept the gradual decline of marital sexuality as a natural development, even though their own ability to reach orgasm remains practically unaffected.

It can be extremely frustrating and distressing especially for women who still have sexual desires, when all intimate physical contact is withdrawn at the same time as sexual relations come to an end – particularly when they (have to) assume that their aging body is the reason for their husband's sexual disinterest. If a couple in such a situation doesn't talk about this problem, they will quickly find themselves caught up in a vicious circle of excuses and insults.

That is why it is extremely important to your relationship that you talk openly about the changing physical conditions. Adjust your attitude towards sexuality to your possibilities and don't put yourself under undue pressure by continually comparing yourself to the 'top performer' of bygone years.

A lot of people find it difficult to talk about their sexual needs and desires. In such cases it can be helpful to start with harmless topics, for example, saying to your partner: "I really like it when you stroke my neck." Once this first hurdle of even talking about physical affection has been taken, it often becomes easier to talk about more intimate details.

Especially couples that get on well with each other in other respects too can quickly overcome the initial shyness of talking about sexual issues.

Try to find appropriate words so that you and your partner can shape your sex life together, even if that might sometimes mean bidding farewell to habits and ideas you've grown rather fond of. Many couples tend to equate sexual experience with sexual intercourse. Indeed, intercourse itself is a substantial part of your sexual relationship. Yet, intercourse and orgasm are not indispensable to fulfilled sexuality.

Mutual explorations of each other's bodies through caresses or massages can be very passionate even without sexual intercourse. Extensive cuddling and some tender loving care can be the fulfilling expression of the intimacy and warmth of a relationship. You can meet your partner's need for love, affection and closeness with loving, gentle touches at least just as well as with acrobatic skills in bed.

Even the widespread problem of slower arousal can turn out to be an opportunity for enhancing a relationship: a woman's arousal curve mostly rises more slowly than a (young) man's in any case. If your partner now also needs longer foreplay to become aroused, you might be able to enjoy some additional tender loving care that you have had to do without up to now, and you will experience physical love all the more intensely… It is not easy to change familiar behavioural patterns. But at every age you have the choice of either changing something or continuing in your well-worn tracks. Breaking the ice is the most difficult part of any form of change. It takes quite a bit of courage to suggest new practices to your partner or to try these out.

On the other hand, it would also be a mistake to want to change everything overnight. However, couples that deal with their sexuality in an open and uninhibited manner, that give each other enough time and that respect each other's speed in attempted changes, can find new means of passionate unity.

In bed, too, consideration, mutual respect and patience are important allies when it comes to solving problems. It is important that you and your partner show each other what is good for you, what you like and which kinds of physical contact you particularly enjoy. Especially when it comes to sex, you should remember that you can't simply anticipate your partner's every desire. By sharing fantasies and talking with each other, even couples who have been together for a long time can positively influence and liven up their love-life anew.

When it comes to love, a general rule is that one partner should not put pressure on the other and should not feel pressurised himself or herself. Affection, attention and intensive empathy for one's partner can help couples to develop a better understanding for each other and to discover those varieties of sexuality and passion that satisfy both partners.

A Suitable Framework

A fulfilled love-life is not a question of age. Decisive is how you shape life together with your partner. Especially long-term relationships have often developed a routine that paralyse mutual attraction. Sometimes, the caring and friendly way in which many couples deal with each other is reminiscent of the way siblings interact. To make sure that love (and not just physical love) isn't snowed under in daily routine, you should try to keep your relationship exciting and sensual.

Routine can quickly lead to boredom and then to disinterest. If, however, you break familiar habits from time to time, the sense of excitement between partners will remain. Imagine a leisurely Sunday morning breakfast for two, with fresh bread rolls and a weekly paper that you share with each other. Such a shared meal is relaxing, calm and peaceful – but not sparkling. Add a bottle of champagne to this scene together with some music, and get rid of the newspaper – and you already have a completely different picture.

This scenario is merely intended to show you how simple it is to add a bit of variety to habitual procedures. Why not allow yourself and your partner a bit of extravagance from time to time – a 'holiday from day-to-day life'? Experiment with what stimulates your sensuality without putting yourselves under pressure.

Candlelight and music or completely new surroundings can create a sensual atmosphere. And if you take a closer look, some daily situations contain a lot of erotic impulses. Try to determine when you find your partner especially exciting and desirable: when showering, cooking, getting dressed or undressing?

Couples that maintain a weekend relationship are likely to be familiar with this phenomenon: when they see each other again after the forced time of separation, they often enjoy being together more than couples who permanently live under the same roof. After all, absence makes the heart grow fonder.

Applied to living together, this means that you should make use of some spare time alone and foster your own interests. If you are aware of yourself as an independent individual, you'll in fact be able to enjoy being close to your partner more consciously. Make sure you do things without your partner every now and then. You will not only be able to bring back new impressions from a visit to the theatre or cinema, or a short holiday alone or with a close friend – this will also provide an opportunity for yourself and your partner to gain some distance from each other and to longingly anticipate your partner's return home.

TANTRA, KAMA SUTRA & CO.

Courses offered in a variety of love techniques promise to (re)kindle sexual desire. The participants in such 'love seminars' are supposed to learn how to rediscover the desire for physical love.

Courses in the ancient Indian teachings of Tantra as a way of harmonising awareness, love and sexuality have recently met with high popular acclaim. Rituals, methods and meditation techniques described in the ancient Hindu writings are supposed to help achieve this. With their assistance, couples learn to form a spiritual unit and complement each other to form a balanced whole. Based on the assumption that sexuality is also influenced by positive vibrations, one of the central teachings of Tantra is that the more love we give, the more love we will receive in return.

A lot of contemporary books describe tantric methods and practices for our modern times. These include various breathing techniques and physical exercises as well as methods that help you to relax, to reduce barriers and to deliberately delay sexual climax. Their application presupposes a certain open-mindedness of both partners towards alternative or esoteric thought patterns.

The Kama Sutra is regarded as the universal manual of sensuality; it is a classic textbook of sensual love. Written roughly two millennia ago, the Kama Sutra assumes that there is a strong connection between you current condition of life, your physical and psychological condition on the one side and your sexuality on the other. A more conscious attitude towards your body is supposed to help people who apply these teachings to find inner peace and balance, while at the same time helping them to experience their sexual feelings all the more intensely. The Kama Sutra also presupposes a certain willingness to deal with topics such as spirituality and your body's energy meridians.

Bon Appétit! Pleasures During Your Meal and Afterwards

A lot of foods are not only very tasty, but are also good for your libido. Why not spoil yourself with an appetising meal: as a starter, maybe some lamb's lettuce with garlic shrimps or Parma ham with melon, as a main course a game dish or a lean beef roast, and for dessert a fruit salad of mango, melon, strawberries and nuts – or perhaps peaches with vanilla ice cream...

When your grandmother used to say that your appetite will come while you're eating, she was probably only thinking about your nutritional habits. But our diet can have a variety of effects on our sexuality, too. A few pounds too many or too few can have a noticeable effect on your libido, and a nutrient deficiency can also make you quite unenthusiastic. A balanced diet that includes a lot of fruit, vegetables and wholemeal products can help deal with this problem.

In eating, just as in love, variety is the spice of life. A caringly prepared meal, an appealingly set table, a glass of good wine and some sensual music can have an appetising effect in more ways than one. But don't eat too much, as a very full stomach isn't very stimulating...

Certain foods are even ascribed a highly positive effect on your libido: these include not only the well-known foods and drinks such as caviar, oysters and champagne, but also other types of seafood, lean beef and venison, asparagus, green leafy vegetables, lentils, fresh parsley and garlic, nuts, egg yolk and milk. Carbohydrates, a major constituent of pasta, for example, provide energy and stamina. Strawberries, melons and mangoes contain the trace element manganese, an important substance which contributes to the body's own production of testosterone and is therefore supposed to have a positive effect on your ability to reach orgasm.

Hot spices also have the reputation of 'heating you up'. Chilli peppers, for example, contain the nutrient capsicain, a substance which not only stimulates the production of the body's endorphins, but also encourages the circulation of blood through the whole body (and therefore also in the sexual organs).

Coffee, alcohol and cigarettes on the other hand are extreme passion-killers. Whereas a small glass of alcohol can have a relaxing and calming effect, too much alcohol reduces your sexual potency. The same applies to caffeine and nicotine.

EXERCISING YOUR PLEASURE MUSCLES

Quite a number of female patients who were advised to carry out special pelvic floor exercises regularly in order to treat incontinence, reported afterwards that their love-life had also significantly improved. Indeed, well trained pelvic floor muscles can make a major contribution to increased sexual pleasure.

Your pelvic floor is made up of three layers of muscles, which are about an inch below your skin and stretch from the pubis to the coccyx. They surround the genitalia of men and women. If the tension in the pelvic floor decreases, this can lead to involuntary release of urine (incontinence) and to a descension of the uterus. But still far too few people are aware that these muscles play an important role in satisfying sexual intercourse. Some therapists even call these muscles the centre of pleasure in the middle of the body.

A few little exercises that you should do daily can help you to train your 'pleasure muscle' and prevent it from slackening. As with any other kind of exercise, the more frequently, regularly and intensively you practise, the more successful you will be.

At first, you should cross your legs when standing, sitting or lying down and firmly press the sides of your feet together. The following exercise is another very inconspicuous but effective one that you can do anywhere and at any time. Tense your buttocks, hold the tension for a few minutes and slowly and consciously relax them again. This exercise should be repeated frequently.

Now, sit on a firm chair and arch your back. Concentrate on the muscles in the lower half of your body and imagine you should close the orifices there. Tense all your muscles when breathing out and release the tension again when breathing in.

Next, sit on the floor. Bend your legs; your lower legs should be apart. Now, use your hands to hold your knees together and try to open your thighs against the resistance of your hands. Breathe out while doing so.

How to Keep Your Soul and Mind Young

As you grow older, do the days seem less fulfilling, are you overcome by sadness more often and do you seem to be getting more forgetful? Then it is high time you took action. After all, there are quite a number of well-known personalities – men and women alike – who show that you can maintain high spirits and can keep your memory fit even at an advanced age.

SELF-CONFIDENCE AND OPTIMISM CAN BE EXERCISED

Are you familiar with that sense of feeling unloved and useless, of simply wanting to be alone, hiding away in bed and ignoring the telephone and doorbell, not wanting to see anyone? Then you are in good company. A lot of women, and to an increasing extent men, regularly go through such moods in the process of aging. No wonder! The media continuously suggest that we only come across as being attractive and desirable when we are young, without a single wrinkle or blemish. But if you sit down and think about this for a moment, you're bound to think of several elderly people who are extremely attractive – not because they look particularly youthful, but because they appear to be self-confident and have a zest for life.

Actually, it's not all that difficult to exercise confidence and to look at life from a more optimistic viewpoint. This is where most people make life unnecessarily difficult for themselves. Instead of living here and now, they constantly look into the future and worry; rather than doing everything they have to do joyfully, they go about unpleasant or monotonous tasks with an attitude of reluctance; instead of taking a positive view of things, they cast a bad light on them. It is hardly surprising that such people are unhappy with themselves.

If you want to become more self-confident and optimistic, you should try to get rid of negative thoughts wherever possible. This is easier said than done – after all, we can't just forget all our worries at once. On the other hand, it is possible to lead a fulfilling life in the face of quite a number of problems. You may even catch yourself exaggerating some problems, which – if you really sit down and try to think about them objectively – are only tiny in reality. It's simply a matter of adopting a new attitude.

LIVING IN THE MOMENT

Have you ever wondered why young children seem extremely happy most of the time, or can stop crying from one moment to the next and start laughing again? They live in the present, in the moment. They don't think about what might happen tomorrow or even in half an hour's time.

Optimistic people find life much easier. Not only can they enjoy the simple things in life much more – they also radiate a natural charisma and have a generally beautiful appearance.

They just accept a situation as it is. Of course, moments of extreme happiness alternate with very unhappy ones, but these are normally overcome very quickly. It would do us all a lot of good if to adopt such a 'childish' attitude to life.

Your are bound to be familiar with such a situation: you can't really enjoy a delicious meal because you keep thinking about the work that is awaiting you afterwards. That's the best way to spoil your enjoyment of life. Simply try to focus on what you are doing at the moment and don't think about what might happen in the next hour, or tomorrow or the day after tomorrow. Of course, this doesn't mean that you shouldn't prepare yourself for important moments of your life, only that you should live in the present and try to enjoy it.

ADOPTING A POSITIVE ATTITUDE

At first sight, most things in life seem neither positive nor negative. Only by looking at them from a positive or negative point of view do they become pleasant or unpleasant. For example, if you begin a certain activity that is basically a fairly neutral one (e.g. cleaning or writing letters) with a negative attitude, you will be unhappy throughout the whole activity. But if you make yourself believe that this activity isn't so unpleasant after all and might even be fun, at least your mood won't change and might even get better. And who knows – at some point, activities you used to hate might actually become enjoyable.

WITH ALL YOUR HEART

People who make a very satisfied impression are normally completely engrossed in what they are doing, regardless of whether it is housework, chatting with friends or negotiating a contract. In future, when you have to do something, try doing it with all your heart and immerse yourself in this activity. In this way, you will firstly achieve better results in your work, which might even earn you some praise (perhaps your own!), and secondly you will find out that you feel much better because you have been fully concentrated on the one activity.

In everything you do, you should remember one thing above all: you can only blame yourself for how you feel – other people might influence your

Don't put off doing unpleasant chores, otherwise they will loom over you like a shadow, whatever else you may be doing. Once you've got around to doing them, however, you will feel very relieved.

feelings, but it is your responsibility whether you make the best or the worst out of a situation. Even if you can't change some situations, at least you can try to change your attitude towards them.

Reinforcing Your Self-confidence

All of the above-mentioned approaches to a more positive attitude to life will simultaneously help you gain greater self-confidence. If you view your life in a positive light, you will also see yourself much more positively. And a positive self-image is a precondition for a healthy sense of self-esteem and a confident appearance.

Believing in Yourself: True Beauty Comes from Within

This is a time-honoured saying. People who are naturally optimistic and self-confident invariably seem to be more attractive – regardless of their age – than people who don't believe in themselves or who walk through life with a negative attitude.

Even people with fairly average looks can appear very attractive. It is their own, personal charisma that makes others ignore shortcomings in their external appearance.

Take the American singer Barbra Streisand, for instance. She never did and still doesn't match the traditional ideal of beauty. Yet, she has millions of fans the world over and an attractive (although no longer very young) husband, who couldn't be accused of being with her only because of her money. Now what made and still makes Barbra Streisand so successful? It is quite simple: she has always believed in herself. At the beginning of her career, hardly anybody would probably have thought she would be able to succeed in show business – her nose simply seemed to be far too big to a lot of people. However, she was successful because of her talent and her will-power – and her prominent nose became one of her distinguishing trademarks. Even when Barbra Streisand directed her first film, a lot of critics were very sceptical – after all, female directors were rare in Hollywood back then, and still are today. Yet, her directing debut also proved to be very successful. Though a lot of very hard work is involved in a career such as Barbra Streisand's, she would probably never have achieved everything she did without a healthy dose of unshakable faith in herself and a fair amount of optimism. Yet most people consider Barbra Streisand to be attractive – even though, or maybe precisely because she doesn't match the traditional notion of beauty. Therefore, true beauty must be related with personality somehow, and not merely with youthful, 'streamlined' looks.

Of course, Barbra Streisand is an extreme example, but there are bound to be a few people among your acquaintances whom you find very attractive even though their outer appearance does not seem particularly appealing at first sight. There might be a person with a very infectious laugh, another might remain confident even in the most difficult situations and a third might be extremely good at listening and giving advice. What they all have in common is that their overall personality or features of their personality that make this particular person seem so attractive. So why shouldn't other people feel the same way about you?

So that's why you shouldn't hesitate to emphasise the most striking features of your personality (the positive ones, of course). If you're uncertain which of these features are the most striking, just ask your friends what it is that they appreciate about you the most. An positive outlook on life and a certain amount of confidence which, in part at least, is a result of your experience and knowledge will contribute towards presenting you in an even better light.

Work on emphasising your positive aspects. Try to not only dispense with negative emotions such as envy or jealousy from your active vocabulary, but also from your behaviour. You will notice that you will immediately become more attractive to others.

WHEN YOUR SOUL IS IN MOURNING: WHAT TO DO ABOUT DEPRESSION

Sometimes, depression sets in for the first time at the beginning of menopause (see chapter two: 'Menopause – an end and a new start'), in which case it is partly a result of the hormone change; but you can be affected by depression at any stage of your life. Up to 20 percent of the population go through a depressive stage at least once during their lifetime. We should provide some clarification for a better understanding: a depression is a psychological illness, in which the patient feels pathologically dejected. Everyone can get depression, no-one is immune to it, not even happy people. That's why no-one can be held responsible for suffering from this illness.

Depression can be the result of serious mental strain (the death of a partner, for example). In this case, scientists talk about reactive depression. Frequently, however, depression sets in for no apparent reason. In this case, the illness is called endogenous (coming from within). A genuine depression has nothing to do with normal fluctuations in mood or 'feeling depressed'. If you suffer from depression, you will feel permanently dejected, can't enjoy anything any longer, and your emotions seem erased. Often you simply feel an emptiness. Chronic tiredness, insomnia, loss of appetite, withdrawal from social life, a reduced sense of self-esteem and feelings of guilt towards other people are common signs of depression. A depression is frequently accompanied by anxiety, as well as thoughts of death or committing suicide.

People suffering from depression are neither able to do anything about this condition themselves, nor are their relatives able to help them. So that is why you should definitely consult a doctor if you suspect depression. This can be your family doctor at first, whom you should give a detailed description of the symptoms, or it can also be a professional psychologist or psychiatrist. As a rule, your family doctor will refer the affected person to a psychologist or psychiatrist: and generally speaking, psychotherapy is appropriate since it can – in some circumstances – prevent a further depression.

Although there are antidepressants available which can alleviate the symptoms and reduce the duration of a depression, the illness itself can unfortunately not be healed by these remedies. In serious cases, medication (lithium) may be used additionally to prevent a relapse. It may be possible some time in the future to produce a medication for healing depression, since scientists suspect that endogenous depression is due to a faulty production of certain chemicals in the brain.

Psychotherapy can be carried out as an in-patient in a clinic, which is particularly appropriate in cases of prolonged depression or suspected suicide attempts. You can also receive therapy as an out-patient, i.e. the affected person has regular appointments with the psychologist and – if circumstances are favourable – can even continue to go about their day-to-day duties.

There are various approaches to therapy which can all be used in treating depression: psychoanalysis, psychotherapy or cognitive-behavioural therapy. These types differ in their methodology. There are also further kinds of treatment, such as Gestalt therapy or therapies focussing on the body, for example therapeutic dancing, which could serve as a supplementary treatment in some cases.

A depression is quite different from a natural feeling of sorrow: the judgement of the person affected is seriously impaired. A person who is in mourning, on the other hand, is able to assess situations that are not related to the cause of mourning in a similar way to people who are not suffering from psychological problems.

If yo
of c
with
citie
diffi
of c

Ge

Tho
rem
St. .
with
sta
tha
brig
be
wo
cou

The
pre
val
you
ph
tec

Ex

Ph
Ev
ha
ple
ho
all
ae
m
be
pl

In psychoanalytic treatment, patients are encouraged to talk about any-thing that comes to their mind or that is worrying them. This is supposed to reveal subconscious conflicts that have existed since childhood and which inhibit development of the personality. The psychological disorder (in this case the depression) is seen as the symptom of such conflicts. According to psychoanalytical theories, once the conflicts have been identified, the patient can start processing them, as a result of which the symptom, i.e. the depression, is healed in the long term.

AFTER A SEPARATION

The partners who are leaving are comparatively well off – they also have to become accustomed to a new life, but they made the decision themselves that they wanted this to happen and possibly even prepared themselves for the separation. The people who are being left generally have greater difficulty in dealing with the separation, especially when it comes out of the blue. It is quite understandable that their world simply seems to collapse at first – everything that was built up together and all plans made for the future are suddenly no longer worth anything. The people who have been left often see no perspective for the future (at least for a brief period of time), especially if they also have to leave behind the flat or house which they shared with their partner for many years. In many cases the costs for the flat or house are too high for one person alone to cover. Women who are unemployed are faced with the question of what they should live from after a separation. Their very existence seems to be threatened.

No wonder a lot of people's first reactions to a separation are feelings of panic, depression and despair. In addition, they are frequently affected by sleeping disorders and a loss of appetite, they feel ugly and unloved and are deeply shaken up emotionally. Frequently, the partners who were left start thinking that the separation was their own fault, which tends to make their self-esteem sink even more. Simultaneously, they tend to feel furious with their partner.

All these feelings are completely normal and are part of the separation process. It takes time to get adjusted to the new situation and to fully accept it. After a while, however, when most of the sorrow has passed, you should start looking ahead once more and concentrate on organising your life anew.

Directly after a separation, it can be helpful to talk with friends, relatives or good acquaintances. If there is no-one in your circle of friends that you can turn to, each city and a lot of charities have counsellors or self-help groups whom you can talk to in order to get things off your chest. Some people also find it very helpful to write down their problems so that they become clearer for them.

In order to strengthen your own self-esteem you should also start doing something for yourself. Maybe a new hairstyle or outfit might be a first step

to helping you feel better? In the long term it would be sensible to take up new activities in which you can find confirmation. This might be taking up a job again, but it could also be doing further training courses or charity work. You will find that you can be very successful in whatever you do if you take care to channel the energy reserved up to then for sorrow, anger, and feelings of guilt into new activities. Of course, you shouldn't suppress your sorrow about the separation, but do try to simultaneously restructure your life and give it a sense of direction again. Meeting new people (as long as you are ready for this) can be very helpful at this stage. You can meet a lot of interesting new people through your job or charity work, but also through leisure activities.

Try to gradually cast off habits that you strongly associate with you partner. If, for example, you always used to take the same route for your walks, try treading new paths. If you always used to get up early on a Sunday in order to be able to 'have more of the day', then why don't you just sleep in for once and treat yourself to breakfast in bed.

After a while, you will also be ready to enter into a new relationship – provided you are interested in one. To seek comfort in the arms of a potential

Finding a new partner at just the right time can help restore your self-confidence.

new partner directly after a separation is usually the wrong way of overcoming the separation.

A Major Upset: the Death of a Partner

It is always very difficult to deal with the death of one's partner, especially if this event was unexpected and there was no chance of mentally preparing for it or saying farewell to the loved one. Regardless of the circumstances of your partner's death, it always takes a long period of time and a lot of energy to live through the time of grief. The bereaved have to go through various stages of mourning, because this is the only way of overcoming their sorrow. In general, the period of mourning is divided into four different stages. During the time immediately after the partner's death, usually lasting several days, the bereaved are under shock, can behave irrationally but can also do what has to be done automatically. In the second stage of mourning, which can last up to six months, the bereaved feel an intense longing for their partner and ask why he or she had to die. In the third stage of mourning, which can also last up to six months, the bereaved tend to be disoriented and don't know what to do with their life now. In the fourth and last stage of mourning, the bereaved finally manage to accept their partner's death and adopt a new outlook on life. The pain starts to fade away.

Whilst there is no remedy for sorrow, there are ways of coping with it better. First of all, it is important to talk with other people about the pain, the anger and all the other feelings storming in on you. Don't be afraid to repeat your story, because this will help you to cope with your emotions. Let your listeners know that it is doing you good to talk about your emotions and your deceased partner, even though it might not seem that way to them at first. Don't be afraid of crying in front of others and letting them comfort you. By allowing your sorrow to run its course, you can better deal with it. If there is no-one in your circle of friends whom you can talk to about your sorrow, look for a self-help group, i.e. a group of people with similar problems. There is bound to be a mourning group in your region (by the way, people not only cry in these groups, but laugh as well).

During the time of mourning, which is an incredible strain on your body, it is important that you pay attention to the little things to improve your general well-being. For example, you should try to get enough sleep, have a balanced diet, and go without cigarettes and alcohol as far as possible. Physical exercise will help as much as conscious relaxation to get rid of the stress that builds up during the mourning process. It can also be very helpful to consciously focus on small things that add beauty to life. This could be a flower by the roadside or a good meal. Even if you might not be able to enjoy it at first, you will gradually train your eye to look out for the beautiful things in life. Allow yourself time to do the things that are good for you. Have a long warm bath, for example, or let yourself be spoilt through a massage or a day at a beauty spa. It might even help you to repeatedly imagine yourself gradually being restored to your former cheerful self. Other positive thoughts about your sorrow (e.g. 'mourning will make me stronger') can also help you to overcome it. Creative activities such as painting a picture, dancing or playing a musical instrument can also help you cope with the loss of a beloved one.

One thing you shouldn't do is to suppress your sorrow, otherwise it will force its way out sooner or later. Suppressed sorrow can lead to depression or other serious physical complaints.

YOUR CHILDREN HAVE MOVED OUT – HOW TO GIVE YOUR LIFE NEW MEANING

Once your own children move out from home and no longer require such close attention, you could start thinking about looking after other people's children.

In general, children nowadays are older when they move out from home than they used to be in former times, but only in rare cases are parents relieved to see their children leave the nest. After all, the relationship between parents and children has also undergone transformation. For most children nowadays, parents are not exclusively people to be respected, but rather their friends. That's also why primarily mothers, who care for the well-being of their children for many years, often to the extent of neglecting their own lives, frequently have mixed feelings about their children moving out. On the one hand, they are happy that their children are able to look after themselves, but on the other hand, the centre of their lives seem to have gone missing once the children move out and they don't know what to do with all the time now on their hands. In certain circumstances this situation can give rise to a fully-fledged depression. So in order to avoid this, you should already start developing new interests and pursuing new activities before your children move out. But even if your children already moved out some time ago, you can of course still find interesting new things to do.

Perhaps now is the right time to discover your hidden talents. In practically every town there is some kind of creative centre where people can paint, make music together or engage in needlework and handicrafts. And these will normally not be just young people, but will represent all age groups. Why not ask your local authority or charity if there is such a meeting place in your area, or whether some institution or other offers courses and workshops on the topics you're interested in? You might even want to take the initiative yourself and start up a new painting or needlework group.

Honorary workers are constantly sought by quite a number of organisations, clubs and institutions. Maybe you have always wanted to do more for animal rights and have only now found the time to help out, for example,

in a home for dogs or cats or join an animal rights organisation fighting for the rights of endangered species? Or perhaps you have a natural talent for organising charity events and jumble sales? There are a number of ways of getting involved in honorary work, and every helping hand is very welcome.

But perhaps none of this interests you in the slightest and you would much rather return to looking after children? Then why don't you advertise your services as a nanny or babysitter – you will not only be doing what you enjoy, but can also earn a little money while doing it.

If you were still working part-time while your children were living at home, you will now have the opportunity to expand your professional activities. Of course, you can also try to return to professional life after an extended break from work, even though this generally tends to become more difficult the older you get. Go to your local job centre and find out about your chances on the current job market. You might even get the opportunity of retraining or expanding on your education. And if you have any talents that are much in demand, perhaps some unusual skills, you can also try to do some freelance or self-employed work. Perhaps you have been enthusiastic about doing pottery for years? Then why don't you sell some of your masterpieces? Can you type quickly? Then you could buy a computer with simple word processing software and offer to take on some writing jobs (you can learn the necessary computer and word processing skills in courses offered by adult education centres). As you can see, you don't need a lot of capital to start a new business, only a bit of courage. And should your business not do as well as expected, at least you won't make a high financial loss.

STRESS MANAGEMENT: GETTING RID OF UNNECESSARY STRESS

The corticosteroid hormones cortisol and cortisone released by the adrenal glands are responsible for the negative physical effects of continuing stress.

Suffering from excessive physical or psychological strain over an extended period not only makes you ill; it also makes you feel much older than you really are – and it will make you *look* much older, too. There is a simple reason for this: when your body is under constant stress, it permanently releases hormones that primarily suppress the activities of the immune system, but also weaken your ability to concentrate. No wonder you become more prone to all kinds of illnesses and feel down and out when you are under constant stress. So it is important to do something about it. There are two strategies you can adpot for dealing with stress: avoid it or reduce it.

AVOIDING STRESS

Of course, the very best way of avoiding stress is to prevent situations from developing that are likely to be stress-inducing. Yet this is easier said than done – because apart from the ability of saying 'no' occasionally, it also requires you to think about yourself and your activities very carefully and possibly even admit to unpleasant truths. After all, a large part of strain does not result from external causes – we often induce the worst stress ourselves.

For example, a married couple is constantly fighting because one of them can't accept the other for what they are. Instead of accepting that your partner can't or doesn't want to change certain habits you get annoyed with them – so you are putting pressure on them (and yourself) and are causing stress. However, if you try to accept your partner as a person with weaknesses and strengths and remember that you aren't perfect either, you can avoid quite a lot of arguments and therefore stress, especially in situations that tend to lead to arguments.

Maybe you are also familiar with the following situation. You know that an important and/or unpleasant task is awaiting you the following day (such as an appointment with your boss, or a complaint). Instead of briefly thinking about how you will behave in the situation and then forgetting about it, you expect the worst. Thoughts like 'The meeting is bound to go pear-shaped', 'People will think I'm an idiot', 'I won't be able to achieve my goals' keep building up. You are causing stress by your thoughts alone, will probably not sleep very well and will have to go to the appointment with a feeling of foreboding. Even if things don't go as badly as antici-pated, you will feel completely exhausted – and look it, too.

Next time, try to think a little more positively. Consciously think back to similar situations that you mastered or, if you have made mistakes in similar situations, think about what you might do differently. After that, you should simply try to clear your mind – ideally with some physical exercise or with the help of a relaxation method. Do something for yourself and pamper yourself. In this way, the type of stress that can make you ill can't even build up.

Do you frequently suffer from stress? Then perhaps you think of yourself as irreplaceable. A lot of people suffering from permanent stress are incapable of delegating work to others, but rather think they have to do everything themselves. If you belong to this group of people, you should learn to assign tasks that can be done just as well by someone else.

One last important thing: learn to say 'no'. A lot of stress is caused by taking on other people's work without previously thinking about how much strain this might place on you. Ask for some time to think about it if you can't make up your mind on the spot, and reject the task afterwards if you think it might overtax you. Should you have a bad conscience about this, remember that other people aren't always there for you either.

REDUCING STRESS

It is not always possible to avoid physical or psychological strain – on some days at work, everything seems to go haywire, and private problems are also not always easy to deal with. If you have that familiar feeling that everything is collapsing around you, just take some time out. This doesn't mean that you should simply abandon the chaos at work (unless you can do so with a good conscience); it means that you must allow yourself some time to deal with the stress once the chaos has subsided.

You can best get rid of stress through physical exercise or with specific relaxation techniques. Why don't you get the old bicycle out again, or go swimming (and to the sauna afterwards) or just take a brisk walk through the woods. Relaxation methods such as autogenous training or meditation are just as effective. They help you to collect your thoughts and you can initially at least forget about your stress or even discard it completely. Chatting with friends can be equally effective: their emotional support can help get rid of stress. A good night's sleep can work wonders, too – more often than not things appear in a completely different light once you've had a good night's sleep. You should make sure to avoid alcohol in stressful situations. Though it might have a calming effect initially, it disrupts your desperately needed sleep and does not contribute towards solving problems.

MEDITATION, AUTOGENOUS TRAINING AND OTHER RELAXATION TECHNIQUES

Try to sort yourself out, get rid of stress and do your body and soul a favour: consciously relax at least once a day using a specific relaxation method. Even if you consider yourself to be one of those people who can best relax in front of the TV or with a good book, you should give it a try at least

How to Overcome Sleeping Disorders

Our sleep can be divided into various stages: light sleep, from which you can easily be woken; deep sleep, from which it is more difficult to be woken; and the dreaming stage, characterised by rapid eye movement (REM).

There is no such thing as *the* sleeping disorder per se: a distinction can be made between difficulties in falling asleep and difficulties in remaining asleep. Falling asleep becomes a problem if it takes longer than half an hour, whereas people who have trouble staying asleep tend to wake up again after less than six hours and can rarely get back to sleep again or can only do so with difficulty. Then there is also insomnia, which sums up all kinds of sleeping disorders that persist for longer than a month.

Sleeping disorders are usually due to psychological causes and are only rarely of a physiological nature. Typically, these are stressful situations in your professional or private life; but factors such as noise, light or an uncomfortable bed can also give rise to sleeping disorders. Likewise, insufficient exercise, excessive consumption of coffee, cigarettes and alcohol, an excessively fatty or rich diet, or working shifts can encourage sleeping

disorders to develop. If you suffer from sleeping disorders, you should try to determine their cause (e.g. if noise is disrupting your sleeping pattern, try to block it out by using ear plugs). The following suggestions can also help you to return to a healthy sleeping pattern and forget about your sleeping disorders.

The first and most important condition for a good and relaxing night's sleep is a bed that matches the needs of your body. You mattress should fit your body in such a way that your shoulders and hips are a little lower than the rest of your body, so as to relieve the stress on your spine. You should get a new mattress roughly every ten years, because your old one will normally be worn out by then.

By the time you go to bed, you should have forgotten about the day's stress. Relaxation techniques and physical exercises can help with this. However, an imaginary journey that you go on in bed can also help you to fall asleep. In addition, you shouldn't start thinking about how you probably won't be able to fall asleep or remain asleep. If you go to bed with positive thoughts ('I'll fall asleep quickly' or 'I'll be able to sleep

Infectious diseases accompanied by a high temperature, pain, heart diseases and coughing attacks or asthma number among the most frequent physical causes of sleeping disorders.

Adhering to a certain routine before going to bed is very favourable for sleep. For example, you might want to shower and brush your teeth shortly beforehand. After that, briefly air your room again before going to bed.

through the night'), you're well on the way to overcoming your sleeping disorder. You should try to have solved problems that worry you (such as arguments with your partner) before going to sleep. If this isn't possible for whatever reason, you could sit down at your desk a couple of hours before going to bed and write down the problem and possible solutions to it. In this way, you can attack your problems before going to sleep and won't have to worry about them in bed.

Don't go to bed unless you really feel tired! If you can't fall asleep yet, there's absolutely no point in going to bed out of principle at 10 p.m. just because you have to get up at 6 a.m. the next day and need your eight hours' sleep. In this case, it is better to go to bed a couple of hours later. You won't be less efficient the next day if you've slept for less than eight hours. If you've gone to bed and notice that you can't fall asleep, it is best to get up again. The same applies if you wake up in the middle of the night and can't go back to sleep; in this case, however, you shouldn't start doing anything exciting, only monotonous and boring tasks that will make you feel sleepy and force you back to bed.

Your bed should only be used for sleeping (or spending some pleasant moments with your partner). Don't put a TV near it and don't keep books on your bedside table – you can watch TV and read in your living room. You shouldn't be watching any too exciting films or reading exciting books immediately before you go to bed anyway, since they will only wind you up. And if you are too excited, you are likely to have difficulty in falling asleep or remaining asleep.

You shouldn't eat anything immediately before going to bed, and your evening meal shouldn't lie heavily on your stomach; but on the other hand, you shouldn't go to bed feeling hungry. Alcohol and cigarettes are best avoided in the evening. Though alcohol might help you to fall asleep, it influences the further stages throughout the night, so that you can't really have a refreshing sleep after drinking alcohol. Similarly, nicotine stimulates your metabolism, increases your heart rate and can thus disturb your sleep.

If you need a sleeping aid, then try valerian or herbal teas. Avoid using sleeping pills, as they could make your problems worse because your body gets accustomed to them and you will soon not be able to fall asleep at all without them. However, teas made from calming herbs or valerian drops generally have very few side-effects or none at all, but still promote sleep. Ask your local chemist for a tea mixture that is suitable for you. The ideal sleeping temperature is 16 to 18°C (61 to 64°F); at lower temperatures, you body is likely to tense up. If you wake up at night with cold feet, you should wear warm socks in bed. And if your partner's snoring is disrupting your sleep, you might want to consider separate bedrooms – or at least wear ear plugs.

My Memory is Deteriorating – But Why?

Be honest now: haven't you often felt rather annoyed about putting something down somewhere and then having to look for it shortly afterwards because you couldn't remember where you'd put it? Do you also have trouble remembering people's names? Do you often find that you even forget what you were just about to say? And do you also have the unsettling impression that your forgetfulness is increasing with age? Then you're not alone, because your brain – just like the rest of your body – is going through the normal process of aging; that's why your memory is gradually deteriorating.

The main reason for our increasing forgetfulness is that nerve cells regularly die off over the course of our lives – either through normal aging processes or through other kinds of damage (e.g. due to alcohol). Nerve cells are the only cells in our body which – when fully developed – are not capable of dividing. This means that nerve cells cannot regenerate and that their supply is thus gradually exhausted.

Further changes in the brain also contribute to a deterioration of our memory: for example, the substances responsible for information transfer are produced in lesser quantities, and the thickness of our brain lobes is reduced. And along with our memory, our reaction time and decision-making capacity are affected. Information can no longer be absorbed and processed as quickly as in younger years.

This may all sound rather unsettling at first, but maintaining a good memory even with progressing age is in fact not at all difficult. All you need is a bit of exercise: just like your body, you can keep your brain fit by means of simple exercises. A possible reason for this is that although more and more nerve cells die as you grow older, new connections between the

Our brain cells die off naturally on a regular basis, but there is no need to expedite this process: limit your alcohol consumption!

nerve cells can be formed at any time. Neurologists believe that the number of connections is in direct correlation with the power of your memory. However, these connections are only formed when you put your brain to work, so especially with progressing years you should start jogging your memory.

HOW TO EXERCISE YOUR BRAIN IN EVERYDAY LIFE

Renowned memory trainers are convinced that the human brain is more capable of taking in information if you endeavour to think in vivid images or pictures. In other words, you should try to come up with mnemonic aids in the form of images for committing important information to memory. If you have difficulties in remembering people's names, for example, you should try to come up with an image that you can easily associate with the appearance of the person when you first hear their name. Maybe a certain Mr. Lyon does in fact bear a resemblance to his feline namesake, or Mrs. Peacock likes to dress very elegantly. Such images can help you to remember names.

The same applies to other types of more abstract information that you have to remember. For example, if you think of things to buy just before you're about to set off to the shops and you don't have the time to add them to your shopping list, it can help to picture them in your mind. When

you are learning foreign vocabulary or difficult words, it is very helpful to come up with mnemonic aids. For example, if you can't remember the difference between stalactites and stalagmites – the spectacular conical limestone formations found in caves – the following might help: stalactites (which hang from the ceiling) have to hold on 'tight' so that they don't fall off, and stalagmites (which form on the ground) 'might' meet them if they grow. All you need is a bit of imagination to come up with such think links, and after a while you will become quite proficient.

You can also develop your pictorial memory in day-to-day life by doing some little mental exercises: look at your desk, your kitchen table or any other table for about one minute, then close your eyes and try to remember what was lying there and in what position. You can easily perform such exercises while going about your housework or other tasks that don't demand highly complex thought patterns. You won't even lose time doing them, as you are exercising your memory alongside your routine activities.

If you like solving crossword puzzles or other riddles, enjoy playing 'Trivial Pursuit' or 'Scrabble', have fun watching quiz shows on television and guessing along with the candidates, you are actively doing something for your memory and obviously having fun at the same time. Card games that demand a lot of concentration can also train your memory (but of course only if you don't drink large quantities of alcohol while playing, as this would damage the nerve cells).

Play more frequently. It's not only a lot of fun, it also stimulates your memory in many ways. If you don't know anybody who likes playing games, why don't you try to find people with similar interests, e.g. by putting a notice in the local paper.

Jogging Your Memory

A lot of people find it very difficult to remember numbers, even though numbers play an important role in our lives – just think of telephone numbers, for example. Why not develop your own system of symbols, where each symbol represents a number from 0 to 9. For example, 0 might be represented by an empty wallet, 1 could be the current Formula One world champion, 2 a married couple, 3 the three wise men, a family could represent number 4 and so on. Of course it is completely up to you which symbol you chose for which number; ideally, you will chose one that has a simple connection to the number. Instead of having to remember someone's phone number in form of individual digits, you can invent a story in which the appropriate symbols occur.

The story matching the number 21 43 01 could for example be the following: A couple meets the Formula One world champion and is completely excited about this. They are joined by a family and the three wise men, whose wallet is empty. Then they all say good-bye to the world champion. Admittedly this isn't a very exciting story, but it is probably easier to remember than the number. Why don't you try it for yourself? Take some telephone numbers that you have difficulties recalling and try to remember them in the form of a short story.

Here's an exercise that will help you improve your memory. The following list always contains three words that are not related in any way. Look at the list for about a minute and try to remember the three terms listed together in each case and the order in which they are listed.

1. kettle – church steeple – telephone card

2. crime novel – horse carriage – onset of winter

3. cowboy hat – laptop – fork

4. candle holder – bouquet of roses – grandfather

5. yoghurt beaker – letter opener – cigarette lighter

6. pack of cards – dog collar – spectacles case

Were you able to remember the individual sequence of terms (in the right order)? If so, congratulations. If not, you should try to come up with short stories to match the different sequences. You can recall these more easily

Think links and pictures can help you remember things. However, thinking in images takes quite a bit of practice.

than the terms on their own. An example for the fourth sequence: a young woman had put a candle into the candle holder and had lit it so that she could see the bouquet of roses she had been given by her beau in the night. But her grandfather came into the room and told her to extinguish the light.

Of course, it takes a bit of practice to be able to think of little stories on the spot, but you will notice how helpful this method can be when you really have to remember something. As a rule of thumb, the more obscure your stories are, the better you are able to remember them. This method can also be used to remember shopping lists and similar such long lists of items.

TEST: HOW FIT IS YOUR MEMORY?

After having already practised a little, here is a short test to help you find out how good your memory actually is. Go through the following exercises, add up your points and then read your evaluation.

1. Look at the following sequences of numbers for three minutes, memorise them and then write them down again from memory:

a) 45 98 74
b) 65 42 56
c) 10 21 01
d) 96 83 21
e) 03 92 17
f) 22 44 85

2. Look at the following shopping lists for two minutes, memorise them and then recite them from memory:

a) stock, ketchup, salami, butter, bread
b) buttermilk, cat food, cheese, olive oil, underwear
c) pasta, pork, gorgonzola, chocolate, baking paper
d) potato crisps, vanilla ice-cream, note paper, TV magazine, ham

3. Look at the following French words for two minutes, memorise them and repeat them from memory:

a) jumeau (twin)
b) loup (wolf)
c) songe (dream)
d) paon (peacock)
e) rutilant (gleaming)
f) scaphandre (wetsuit)
g) morceau (piece)

Evaluation:

Give yourself one point for every correct answer.

With a total of 0–6 points your memory is far from performing as well as it could. You should challenge it more by performing regular memory exercises – ideally, you should practise about 15 minutes per day.

If you managed to get 7–13 points, your memory is already working quite well. Even if you have already been exercising it, don't give up – your memory can still improve.

Did you get 14–17 points? Well done! Your memory is still in very good working order. Don't leave it at that though: continue to exercise it, to keep it in good shape.

Index